ROUTLEDGE LIBRARY EDITIONS: THE LABOUR MOVEMENT

Volume 1

LABOUR IN LONDON

LABOUR IN LONDON
A Study in Municipal Achievement

BRIAN BARKER

LONDON AND NEW YORK

First published in 1946 by George Routledge & Sons. Ltd.

This edition first published in 2019
by Routledge
2 Park Square, Milton Park, Abingdon, Oxon OX14 4RN

and by Routledge
711 Third Avenue, New York, NY 10017

Routledge is an imprint of the Taylor & Francis Group, an informa business

© 1946 Brian Barker

All rights reserved. No part of this book may be reprinted or reproduced or utilised in any form or by any electronic, mechanical, or other means, now known or hereafter invented, including photocopying and recording, or in any information storage or retrieval system, without permission in writing from the publishers.

Trademark notice: Product or corporate names may be trademarks or registered trademarks, and are used only for identification and explanation without intent to infringe.

British Library Cataloguing in Publication Data
A catalogue record for this book is available from the British Library

ISBN: 978-1-138-32435-0 (Set)
ISBN: 978-0-429-43443-3 (Set) (ebk)
ISBN: 978-1-138-32440-4 (Volume 1) (hbk)
ISBN: 978-1-138-32447-3 (Volume 1) (pbk)
ISBN: 978-0-429-45087-7 (Volume 1) (ebk)

Publisher's Note
The publisher has gone to great lengths to ensure the quality of this reprint but points out that some imperfections in the original copies may be apparent.

Disclaimer
The publisher has made every effort to trace copyright holders and would welcome correspondence from those they have been unable to trace.

LABOUR IN LONDON

A STUDY IN MUNICIPAL ACHIEVEMENT

By
BRIAN BARKER

With a Foreword by
LORD LATHAM

LONDON
GEORGE ROUTLEDGE & SONS, LTD.
BROADWAY HOUSE : 68–74 CARTER LANE, E.C.

First published 1946

THERE is now a general recognition that the town or city is not a remote abstraction with which the citizens have no personal concern, but an important factor in their associated lives, and that upon the wise direction of its common affairs the happiness and prosperity of the inhabitants in great part depend.

        LORD SNELL,
            Chairman of the London County Council.
                            1934–1938.

THIS BOOK IS PRODUCED IN
COMPLETE CONFORMITY WITH THE
ECONOMY STANDARDS

Printed in Great Britain by Butler & Tanner Ltd., Frome and London

CONTENTS

CHAP.		PAGE
	FOREWORD by LORD LATHAM	vi
I	"VESTED INTERESTS IN DIRT AND DISEASE"	1
II	THE STRUGGLE FOR MUNICIPAL REFORMS	28
III	THE RISE OF THE LONDON LABOUR PARTY	53
IV	THE GOVERNMENT OF LONDON	68
V	CLEARING AWAY THE SLUMS	83
VI	A GREAT EXPERIMENT IN SOCIAL WELFARE	112
VII	A MUNICIPAL HEALTH SERVICE	134
VIII	PROGRESS IN EDUCATION	152
IX	PEACE AND PROGRESS	163
X	LONDON GOES TO WAR	181
XI	REST CENTRES AND EMERGENCY FEEDING	195
XII	EDUCATION IN WARTIME	203
XIII	SOCIAL WELFARE IN WARTIME	210
XIV	WAR OVER THE HOSPITALS	218
XV	THE LABOUR BOROUGHS OF LONDON	227

FOREWORD

By LORD LATHAM, *Leader of the London County Council.*

MR. BRIAN BARKER has written a clear and concise account of the march of Labour to the control of the London County Council and of its work at County Hall. It is a story of clarity and firmness of purpose : of sustained and planned progress to victory, and then of solid and sound achievement in the administration of the greatest municipal authority in the world. In peace and in war the Labour Majority on the County Council has shown itself capable of the efficient and progressive government of London. The written proof is to be found in the impressive record set out in the pages of this useful and factual study. The actual proof can be seen wherever the vast and complex activities of the L.C.C. take place, both within the County and outside. Yet the living testimony resides in the knowledge and appreciation of the great people of London that Labour kept its promises to them in the short years of peace and sustained, helped and comforted them in the dark and dangerous years of war.

It is not my purpose in this foreword to go over the ground covered by the Author, but rather to set out in broad outline some of the developments we shall seek to carry out in the future. The speed and the measure of our progress in these will depend to an appreciable extent upon factors which are outside our control : such as the availability of labour and materials ; adequate powers and reasonable financial assistance from central funds. Nevertheless, the Labour Majority at County Hall will not rely upon these factors as excuses for inaction, but will press on with every energy and resource at its command. Nor will it depart from its established practice and tradition of not making promises it cannot fulfil.

The London County Council faces the immense task of repairing the widespread damage done to its houses, flats, schools, hospitals and many other public buildings, and the replacement of those destroyed. In addition, the removal of blast-walls and other protective work and the re-adaptation of buildings which have been used for civil defence purposes will be a big job. Furthermore, there are six years of accumulated arrears of maintenance to be tackled as speedily as possible, in order to restore the amenities of schools, hospitals and the like. All this work of repair, restoration and replacement will compete for labour and materials which are and will be for some time in short supply : they will compete not only between themselves, but with the need for construction of new houses, flats, new schools and new hospitals. In the field of new construction, housing must come first, but hard on its heels will be the need for new schools, not only to replace those destroyed, but also those which are outworn and out of date and, moreover, to provide school accommodation in those areas where, owing to the shift of population, it is insufficient. The number of additional school places required will be increased by the higher standard of amenity and the smaller classes essential if improved educational facilities are to be available for our children.

Against this background of competing urgencies, what developments has the Labour Majority in mind for the future ? First, it has resolved that reconstruction must be according to the ordered principles of sound, long-term planning. The Council has therefore adopted the main principles of the County of London Plan and will, as regards its own building, seek to conform with them : it will also endeavour to guide and direct private development along lines which accord with these principles. The extent to which it can do the latter will depend on the Council having wider powers, and not less so upon the burden of compensation being borne by the Exchequer. Planning the physical and social lay-out of London is a long-term job and can only be carried out in a series of stages which can be self-contained and yet fall into the general pattern of the comprehensive plan as one organic whole.

On the 17th July 1945 the Council decided to approve the general principles of the County of London Plan and

that the attack on London's four major defects (traffic congestion, depressed housing, intermingling of housing and industry, and insufficiency of open space) should be opened in the immediate future—

(1) by embarking on a short-term programme of road works of the highest priority;
(2) by commencing operations of re-development in certain reconstruction areas in the County of London, particularly the area in Stepney and Poplar;
(3) by initiating re-development in the area on the south bank of the Thames between Westminster bridge and Waterloo bridge;
(4) by concentrating (as a step towards the achievement of an ultimate standard of 4 acres of open space per 1,000 population) on the acquisition and reservation of sufficient land to increase to $2\frac{1}{2}$ acres per 1,000 population open space in those areas where at present the provision falls short of that amount.

Although only part of the first stages, these projects taken together constitute an immense job, greater than anything ever before contemplated by the London County Council or any other local authority. They are additional to a big and sustained programme of housebuilding, both within and without the County. In our legitimate zeal for planning we must be careful not to impede or slow down our attack on London's acute shortage of dwellings or the removal of its slums by providing the maximum number of dwellings in the minimum of time.

In Education the Council will bend all its efforts to squeeze out of the new Education Act every ounce of educational advance and improvement : primary, secondary and continuation. This will be a great and beckoning task. There are many obstacles in the path, including the embarrassing legacy of many out-worn and out-moded school buildings. We shall overcome them wherever possible. In the sphere of providing secondary education the Council has already adopted the principle of Multilateral Schools for London children from the age of eleven. In these comprehensive high schools invidious distinctions between types of secondary schools will disappear and parity of esteem and a common interest and associated school life in one educational unit will be sought. Pending the erection of new schools of this character, the Council has decided that, so soon as after-war conditions permit, existing school units should be grouped on an area basis to form a comprehensive high school unit, in which premises, equipment, amenities and activities would be shared in common. These decisions of the Council have earned the plaudits of instructed educational opinion, and it is no exaggeration to say that in adopting these bold and far-reaching proposals the Labour London County Council has blazed a trail which may become a broad avenue leading towards equality of education throughout this County.

The Council is considering post-war reorganization and development of its hospitals and health services. Until the shape of the proposed National Health Service is known it is impossible to lay down definitely the lines this will follow. Suffice it to say that the Labour

Majority, which since 1934 has done so much to improve London's hospital services, will be resolute to provide the best and most up-to-date system of hospitals and medical services it can for the people of London, and will seek to secure the fullest benefits from the comprehensive national health service when established.

These are the main, but by no means the only developments and projects we on the London County Council have in mind or are actively considering. All the services of the Council will be reviewed in the light of the broadening needs of the future. If any proof be needed of the Labour Party's will and capacity to use the varied and widespread services of the London County Council for the betterment of London and for the enrichment of the lives of its people, such proof is to be found in abundant measure in the impressive array of facts which Mr. Brian Barker has presented in this book.

LABOUR IN LONDON

Chapter I
" VESTED INTERESTS IN DIRT AND DISEASE "

It might be claimed that Britain is a country where a revolution can slip in by the back door.

The pace of social and economic progress in Britain has indeed been swifter than we sometimes suspect. It is no exaggeration to say that the life of our people has been transformed in the last hundred years. The gap between social conditions in 1840 and the present day is almost as wide as the gulf between savagery and civilisation.

One hundred years ago the expectation of life in one of the big towns in Britain was about twenty-six years. Only one child out of every three grew up to the age of five. Smallpox laid its deadly and disfiguring touch on the great majority of the population of these islands. One hundred years ago nearly every person was either recovering from or sickening for enteric fever. In 1840 over 14,000 people died from cholera in London alone.

We have stamped out smallpox and cholera, and the once universal enteric fever today is responsible for less than six in a million deaths. The death-rate from tuberculosis, diphtheria and other infectious and deadly diseases has been cut to an extent which would have been considered impossible by the disease-harried generation of a hundred years ago.

The dweller in the worst slum existing in Britain today enjoys amenities undreamed of by the ordinary citizens of London a hundred years ago. Numerous descriptions of the state of London at this time exist; they all have the same features. The ordinary citizens of London lived in miserable houses surrounded by a morass of filth and mud. There was no obligation on landlords to keep their houses in decent repair or to prevent them being overcrowded; there was nothing to prevent any sort of hovel being used as a human dwelling. Thousands of new houses were rushed up to meet the needs of a population which, in London, had doubled itself in less than forty years. Most of these houses were small, badly built, huddled together and were without even elementary sanitation. The window tax imposed toward the end of the eighteenth century was not repealed until 1851, so that for fifty years Parliament gave a direct encouragement to building houses with the least possible enjoyment of light and air.

No proper means were provided for the disposing of refuse. Chadwick, the great sanitary reformer of the times, reports,

Many of the streets in which cases of fever are common are so deep in mire, so full of holes and heaps of refuse, that the vehicles used for conveying patients to the house of recovery cannot be driven along them and patients are obliged to be carried to it from considerable distances.

London was honeycombed with cesspools of which some were so large that they were described as cesslakes. Many of the cesspools leaked into the water supplies. The few sewers which existed discharged their untreated contents into the Thames, which became " a foul, foetid ditch, its banks coated with a compound of mud and filth and strewed with offal and carrion ". This condition did not deter many of the water companies which gave London its fitful supplies from drawing their water from the Thames within the metropolis and

" Vested Interests in Dirt and Disease "

delivering it unfiltered and unpurified. It was not until 1852 that Parliament was induced to compel the water companies to take their supplies from above Teddington Lock, and to filter it.

London and the other great towns of Britain were growing up unplanned, uncontrolled, a morass of rotten housing and indescribable filth, in which every small and big speculator could follow his own private interests without regard to the health, convenience or welfare of every other citizen in the community. It was the golden age of " free " enterprise. It must indeed have seemed, as Corbusier says, that the cities were growing up to be a " disaster to mankind ".

A society which paid such scanty attention to the physical welfare of human bodies devoted even less attention to the needs of the human mind. The level, exact phrases of Sidney Webb can perhaps best convey some idea of the conditions under which the children of London lived less than a hundred years ago. There were over a half million children in London who were

growing up not only practically without schooling or religious influences of any kind, but also indescribably brutal and immoral : living amid the unthinkable filth of vilely overcrowded courts unprovided either with water supply or sanitary conveniences, existing always at the lowest level of physical health and constantly decimated by disease ; incessantly under temptation by the flaring gin palaces which alone relieved the monotony of the mean streets and dark alleys to which they were doomed ; graduating almost inevitably into vice and crime amid the now incredible street life of an unpoliced metropolis.[1]

Little more than seventy years stand between us and the illiterate barbarity of the London which Sidney Webb describes. We have travelled fast and far in the span of

[1] Sidney Webb, *London Education*, p. 4. 1904 edition.

a single lifetime. To acknowledge that fact is not necessarily to grow complacent about the needs of the present. Those who recognise the revolutionary changes of the past century will be the most eager to press forward in the great tradition of progress and reform.

While it may not stir our political imaginations it is very necessary to recognise that the superstructure of civilisation rests on the provision of pure water, good drains and clean streets. It is only when we possess these sanitary necessities that healthy and civilised life in urban communities becomes at all possible. Furthermore, the enormous development of industry, with the vast output of factory-produced commodities and steadily rising standards of living, has become possible not only because we are a healthy but also a literate people.

Water, drains, roads and education, these are the province of our system of local government, and it was the provision of a better system of local government which cleaned up these Augean stables of filth and disease which were our towns and cities less than a hundred years ago. It was the local authorities which brought education and a civilising influence into the brutal jungle of the London slums. It would be the height of political foolishness to focus attention exclusively on the " high policies " of Parliament and to overlook the struggle which has gone on around the parish pump. The struggle for better local government was—and still remains—a struggle for the means of carrying civilisation forward.

In the later pages I have attempted to record, as impartially as I can, what the London Labour Party's control of the machinery of local government has meant for the people of the County of London. We shall see that even after a hundred years there still remained a vast job to be done in improving London's sewers. There were still areas of London, and whole fields of administration where, after a fast spurt towards the end of the century, the pace of improvement and reform had then moved very slowly and sluggishly indeed. There was still a great deal to be done for the educational and health services in London. There was, when Labour came into power, still vast scope for the civilising influence of an efficient and humane system of civic administration.

The social pressures and political influences of the past hundred years have determined the quality and efficiency of the machinery of our present civic administration. This is especially true of London, where the machinery of local government is very different from, and possibly less efficient in its form, than that possessed by any other great urban centre in Britain. In London, even today, there is too often not only a task to be done, but also a struggle to adjust the machinery to the task. In order that much in the following pages may be intelligible it is, then, necessary to glance, very briefly, at the development of local government in London.

Many of the English counties have boundaries which are the same as those of the ancient kingdoms carved out by Saxon and Danish conquerors. But London alone of all the counties and cities of Britain carries forward in its very heart the fossilised form of medieval government. The ancient but tenacious core of the metropolis, known as the Corporation of the City of London, has been the barrier which has broken much of the impetus towards improvement and reform in the government of the metropolis. The wealth and influence which find expression in the ancient pageantry of the Livery Companies and the Lord Mayor were still as powerful to resist municipal progress in the twentieth century as they were to resist the encroachments of kings and parliaments in the long centuries of London's history. It is possibly not without significance that wealth and privilege are thus still powerfully and ostentatiously entrenched at the very centre of the British community and Empire.

Yet the City of London in its beginning was one of the earliest and most democratic assemblies of which we have record. In Saxon times the people of London came hurrying to the common assembly, the folk moot, to the clang of the bell of ancient St. Paul's. The aldermen who controlled the city's life were elected in that popular assembly. Vestiges of that early democracy are still enshrined in the gilded paraphernalia of the City today.

For many centuries the citizens of London were always in the van of the fight against the feudal claims of the Crown. But as London grew in influence and power, so there commenced to creep in amongst the freemen the tendency to confine the right of citizenship to the favoured few. More and more the popular struggle against the claims of a feudal autocracy was changed into the struggle of a newly rising class of merchant princes to protect their wealth and extend their influence. The popular influence in the government of London declined as the wealth accumulated in the hands of the great merchants of the City of London.

At some undecided date in those early centuries the Guilds and Livery Companies were grafted into the government of London. Originally, the Guilds possessed important social and economic functions. They exercised control over their members and protected the public from the sale of fraudulent goods; they protected their members from unfair competition and decided what should be the qualifications for the right to practise the craft, and they regulated the conditions of apprenticeship. Finally, and most important, the guilds provided a sort of friendly society to which vast sums were contributed by the members for the sick and old members of the company, and for the education of their children.

"Vested Interests in Dirt and Disease"

With the rise of modern industrialism, the economic functions of the guilds sank into disuse. They still retained, however, their vast funds derived mainly from the investments in increasingly valuable property in the City and from other estates. And they still continued to exercise their political powers. The liverymen of the Companies of the City of London, with the aldermen of the Corporation, form the Court of the Common Hall which selects two aldermen, one of whom the aldermen themselves choose for Lord Mayor, and the sheriffs and other officers who still exercise important judicial and administrative duties in the City of London. Thus the Lord Mayor, who claims to be the foremost citizen and principal spokesman of the teeming millions of London, is the nominee of less than 10,000 liverymen, the majority of whom have no special knowledge or interest in the welfare of Londoners or their government.

However, the main purpose of this brief sketch of the Corporation of the City of London is not necessarily to cavil at its wealth, its influence, or its ancient privileges. We are concerned here with its influence on the development of London's system of local government. And the extent of that influence cannot be ignored. At this distance of time it is difficult to assess contemporary motives, but it is perhaps fair to assume that at a very early stage in the transition from democratic assembly into the closed corporation of the City of London the leading members must have recognised that to extend the boundaries of the City means also to increase the pressure of popular demand for a share in its government. Bigger territory might also involve a bigger franchise, " The boundaries of the City were fixed at an early date and there is no record of their ever having been enlarged to correspond with the growing size of the town." [1]

[1] Royal Commission on the City Corporation of London, 1854.

London grew steadily all through the centuries, with sudden great spurts of building at the Renaissance, again after the Great Fire of 1666, and yet again with catastrophic suddenness at the beginning of the new industrial age. Neither plague, nor fire, nor the edicts of Elizabeth and James I could stem the great tide of growth. During all those centuries the City stood fast on its own boundaries, maintained its own system of relatively efficient self-government and ignored the problems of the swelling conglomeration beyond its walls whose inhabitants were utterly without any coherent form of municipal government.

From the beginning the wealthy members of the City had seen the threat to their privileges which was inherent in any extension of its borders. But the steady growth of London was bringing larger national consequences in its train. This great reservoir of human beings, many of them restless and debased by extreme poverty, might easily become a threat to every established institution in the kingdom. There had been times when the atomised units of London had suddenly coalesced under the pressure of unendurable poverty or dire repression. There had been moments when the twisted fingers of poverty had suddenly gripped privilege itself by the throat. And the Kings, the Lords, the landowners and merchants in Parliament or in Common Hall assembled had remembered that experience and could shrewdly estimate that in the great mass of London was a latent power which, if it found the enduring determination, could swiftly shake the whole foundations of society. The inference was obvious. To create a central system of civil government in London might well mean establishing in concrete form a threat which was still dispersed over a large number of small and ineffectual units.

We have touched here on one of the enduring patterns

in the relations of the people of the capital with the central authority of the State. The distrust and apprehension with which the central authority has regarded any extension or consolidation of the popular influence in London makes clear much that would otherwise be obscure in London's history. It has been largely responsible for moulding the structure of local government in London on the basis of a division of local powers. To a considerable extent it has, as we shall see, determined the machinery by which many of the capital's public services are operated. This same distrust and apprehension put its stamp on the early London County Council. It drove the Progressives from power in London, and confronted the London Labour Party when it stepped forward to take up the task of government.

By the beginning of the nineteenth century the City's policy of exclusiveness and Parliament's distrust of the people had worked their worst for London. The City, now the undoubted citadel of wealth and influence, enjoyed within its square mile the efficient administration of a municipal corporation. Beyond its walls, the vast mass of London, with a population eight times as large, had a system of local government equivalent, at its best, in scope and efficiency to that possessed by a number of scattered rural parishes.

The capital's government, like the destitute, rested on the only support available—the parish with its annual vestry meeting. In the case of the open vestry there was some pretence of popular representation, and the inhabitants at the annual meeting elected the local constable, who kept order, the surveyor to look after the roads, and the overseer of the poor to look after the destitute. But there was an even worse form of government than the open vestry, which at least did make some pretence to popular government. The close or select vestry confined the rights of attending the parish meeting to a select few, or allowed the members to co-opt new members as vacancies occurred. There were many vestries of this form in London, and the opportunities it gave to corruption were unlimited. Vast sums of public money vanished into private pockets. The poor were neglected, the highways were filthy, unpaved and infested with thieves.

But there were areas of London where there was not even this slender pretence of self-government.

In many places, and notably in districts which had become densely peopled with the poorest of the poor, there was not even a pretence of management, no public or quasi-public body existing at all for any sanitary purposes. And where there were such bodies their administration was usually a mere mockery of local government, the only reality of which was its entire freedom from control and its consequent inefficiency and extravagance. Miscellaneous bodies of paving commissioners, lighting commissioners, turnpike boards, directors of the poor, etc., were scattered at random over the town without regulations for their guidance, no attempt at uniformity of administration, no bond of union, no security for the proper performance of their functions. In most cases these bodies were entirely self-elected, and even where in theory the ratepayers were the electors, the process of election was conducted in a hole-and-corner fashion, and was utterly corrupt.[1]

London remained outside of the cleansing reforms which were sweeping away the narrow and inefficient system of local government in the rest of the English towns. The Reform Act of 1832 was on the Statute Book. The new middle classes of the towns were enfranchised and they were not disposed to see the town corporations dominated by Tories and Anglicans. The merchants and manufacturers who had brought wealth to

[1] J. F. B. Firth, *The Reform of London Government* (1888), p. 40.

the towns objected to a self-perpetuating oligarchy in local government which imposed all sorts of restrictions on the freedom of trade and manufacture. Accordingly, the Whig Government had very good reasons for reforming the boroughs. They appointed a Royal Commission whose recommendations formed the basis of the Municipal Corporations Act of 1835. The closed corporations which had run the towns gave place to municipal councils elected by the whole of the ratepayers, while arrangements were made to extend their boundaries over the adjoining areas where people had spilled out of the original towns.

Local government in the provinces was fairly radically transformed. But London remained outside the sphere of reform, although the Commissioners who had recommended the legislation for the provincial towns had insisted that a similar measure of reform should be introduced in the metropolis. They reported that " we do not find any argument on which the course pursued with regard to other towns could be justified which does not apply with the same force to London ". They took a firm stand on the exclusive privileges claimed by the City. " We are unable to discover any circumstances justifying the distinction of a small area within the municipal boundary from the rest, except the fact that it is, and long has been, so distinguished." [1] They specially insisted on the unity of London, and dismissed as likely to multiply evils the suggestion that London should be split up into a number of communities. They emphasised the importance of the central administration of paving, sewage and the lighting of streets, " which it seems to us can never be so economically and efficiently performed in one town as when superintended by one undivided authority ". They roundly condemned the

[1] Royal Commission on Municipal Corporations (1837), Second Report.

Labour in London

"Common Hall" which, as we have previously noticed, selects the Lord Mayor and Sheriffs of London.

Supposing that any useful purpose is served by such an assembly, we know of no circumstances justifying this restriction to the Livery. . . . There is at present a manifest absurdity in attaching political and municipal privileges to the nominees of the Corporations which claim to be private, independent of the City and irresponsible.[1]

It is perhaps worth commenting that the "manifest absurdity" still exists to the present day. As for the report of the commissioners, it was not the first, or the last, time that the report of a Royal Commission was shelved in face of the powerful and implacable opposition of the City and the stubborn resistance of the House of Lords.

For another eighteen years the chaos and corruption in London's government continued. By 1841 it was estimated that the 270,859 houses in the metropolis were fitted with 300,000 cesspools.[2] The main natural drainage artery of London, the Thames, had become the main sewer. The streets of Bermondsey were described by its medical officer as a "disgrace to the civilised world". In Whitechapel there was neither drainage, sewerage, cleansing, paving nor a good supply of water. Slaughter-houses, pigsties, and such noxious trades as bone-boilers and manure manufacturers poured their stench into the air and their effluents into the soil and open drains. The dead were buried in overcrowded grounds surrounded by houses. Chadwick in his report to the Government on the sanitary conditions of London stated that

In the metropolis, on spaces of ground which do not exceed 203 acres, closely surrounded by abodes of living, layer upon

[1] Royal Commission on Municipal Corporations (1837), Second Report.
[2] Third Report of the Metropolitan Sanitary Commission, 1848.

"Vested Interests in Dirt and Disease"

layer, each consisting of a population numerically equivalent to a large army of 20,000 adults and nearly 30,000 youths and children, is every year imperfectly interred. Within the period of the existence of the present generation upwards of a million dead must have been interred in these same spaces.

A graver threat than social revolution was beginning to rear itself on the corrupt and chaotic administration of London. Asiatic cholera exercises very little class distinction in the selection of its victims, and the outbreaks of this dread plague were becoming more frequent and more deadly. The reports of Chadwick, Southwood-Smith, Kay and many other sanitary reformers had shown the connection between filth and disease. A Metropolitan Sanitary Commission which reported in 1847 emphasised the desirability of combining the control of the water supply with control of the drainage, sewage and refuse-disposal services. In 1848 there was another violent outbreak of cholera, and an alarmed Parliament was driven to pass hurried legislation.

An Act was passed to consolidate and unify the inefficient commissioners of sewers—there were 1,065 of them—except, of course, those operating in the City. Twelve commissioners were appointed to keep the sewers in order and to make new ones for " effectually draining the area within the limits of the Commission ". The effect of this limitation was that the new body had no power to provide for the removal of sewage from the neighbourhood of London to a more remote place. This ineffectual Commission was soon succeeded by another equally impotent body. Altogether, no less than six Commissions of Sewers were appointed in six years without any of them being able to work any important improvement in the metropolitan sewers.

Cholera and other infectious diseases pursued their deadly way among the inhabitants of the metropolis. A severe outbreak of fever attacked the boys of Westminster School as a result of the defective sewers and cesspools in the precincts of the Abbey. The stench from the Thames had grown to such an extent that it reached the nostrils of the honourable gentlemen themselves, driving them from the library and committee rooms and pursuing them inexorably into the Chamber. The very air of London was reeking with an urgent message of reform.

But there was also another message in the air. One that Parliament found equally pervading and insistent—the deep and swelling clamour of the outraged ratepayers of London. The whole administration of the capital was falling still further into the grossest corruption. Public money was disappearing into private pockets on a fantastic scale. The immense hotchpot of Paving Commissioners, Lighting Commissioners, Directors of the Poor, Turnpike Boards and other bodies were, in many cases, lavishly enjoying the fruits of office, voting themselves fees and expenses on a magnificent scale, and farming out contracts among themselves and their friends. All over London the good hard cash of the ratepayers was supporting a hoard of corrupt officials and their underlings, while the roads remained unlighted, unpaved and filthy, the cesspools leaked into the water supplies, and the grossest inefficiency and corruption became the hallmark of local government in the metropolis.

At various times during the first half of the century, the clamour for the reform of the vestries and the commissioners had become loud and insistent. But the popular demand had always been broken by the implacable refusal of Parliament to remedy the abuses or give London a coherent system of local government. Many of the vestries, boards and commissions had buttressed their inefficiency and corruption by appointing

"Vested Interests in Dirt and Disease"

guinea-pig members from among the nobility and peerage. In St. Giles-in-the-Fields, the Close Vestry included not only many peers but also two Chief Justices and two other judges.[1] " We have always ", said a Marylebone vestryman in 1830, " made a point of having as many noblemen and members of Parliament as we could get hold of." [2]

The tentacles of corruption were reaching deep into the body of society. The question of the reform of the government of the metropolis had become inextricably interwoven with the prestige and profits of the peerage, the judges and the members of Parliament themselves. In the circumstances it is hardly surprising that the attempts at reform received short shrift. For example, when the ratepayers of St. Pancras brought forward two Bills with the object of remedying the abuses of the paving boards, Parliament curtly rejected the Bills which had cost the ratepayers £4,000 to promote, " and the paving boards, over which the ratepayers had no control, spent nearly £3,000 in defeating the ratepayers, which the ratepayers had likewise to pay ".

By the middle of the century, however, the pressure for reform was too strong to be turned aside. Sanitary reformers, clergymen appalled by the corrupt use made of their vestries, and middle-class citizens whose rates disappeared without leaving a vestige of public service behind, were united in their determination for reform. The pamphlets poured in a spate from the printing presses. Reforming societies, some of them claiming a half-million members, sprang up all over the metropolis. The Riot Act was read at Vestry meetings when stolid and respectable ratepayers tried to oust the ruling

---

[1] S. & B. Webb, *English Local Government : The Parish and the County*, p. 213.
[2] First Report of House of Commons Committee on Select Vestries, 1830.

oligarchy by force. Finally, the cholera preached to rich and poor alike, to Parliament and ratepayers, its grim lesson of the terrible consequences of the continuance of anarchy, corruption and chaos in the government of the metropolis.

It was not by Government enactment, however, but by a private member's Bill that London at last secured some semblance of coherent control over the vital public services. In introducing his Metropolitan Management Bill, Sir Benjamin Hall, himself a former Health Commissioner, gave a summary of the management of London in 1855. London, he said, had a population of 2,333,100 living in 291,240 houses, and the rateable value, excluding the City of London, was just over nine million pounds. The number of different local acts setting up various local boards and commissions was 250, independent of the general acts administered by no less than 300 different bodies. He estimated that the metropolis was governed by no less than ten thousand commissioners.

His speech was a long indictment of the inefficiency, chaos and corruption which had gripped the capital. He mentioned the Strand Union with its eleven miles of streets divided up among seven paving boards, each with its staff of clerks, collectors, surveyors and other officers, and to show what manner of officers were appointed, he observed that one of the surveyors was a tailor and the other a law stationer. Between the Strand and Temple Bar, a distance of little more than a thousand yards, the street was divided into seven different paving boards. In St. Pancras it was costing the ratepayers £5,000 a mile to repair the roads. In quiet phrases he went on to give instance after instance of the gross inefficiency, open corruption and the chronic anarchy which had overtaken the government of the greatest city on earth.

The Metropolitan Management Act of 1855 passed

the House of Commons, possibly, because it represented a cautious compromise with all the large and small vested interests concerned with the government of the metropolis. The City remained untouched in all its wealth and territorial integrity. Those antique encumbrances, the parish vestries, still remained the basic units of municipal administration. Under the Act some of the smaller parishes were grouped into fifteen districts, administered by district boards, and these indirectly elected boards, together with the larger vestries, became responsible for electing a central body called the Metropolitan Board of Works. The limited objectives of this Board were clearly indicated in the preamble to the Statute which declared that the Act was passed in order to make provision " for the better management of the metropolis in respect of the sewerage and drainage and the paving, cleansing, lighting and improvements thereof ". Thus the narrowest possible view was taken of the Board's functions. It was stunted in the very act of birth. A municipal dwarf was expected to govern the immense urban conglomeration of London.

The aim of the Act of 1855 was to govern London through the localities, with the vestry as the responsible body. The Metropolitan Board, consisting merely of representatives of the vestries, was to be their servant, carrying out work on their behalf. But the unity of London proved too strong for this idea, and as new services were required they were entrusted to the central authority. The Board, with all its limitations, had stepped into the vacant centre of metropolitan government, and there was an almost irresistible impulsion to make it the authority for administering the new services which were developing in London. Thus, the Metropolitan Board took over the inspection of the gas supply in 1860, and became responsible for organising the first effective London fire service in 1866; in the ensuing years further powers were added to the Board, including the responsibility for providing parks and open spaces, slum clearance, and the collection of a rate to defray the cost of relieving the casual poor.

But these new powers were cautiously and grudgingly conferred. Furthermore, Parliament carefully sowed the seeds of division and conflict by appointing new bodies to deal with matters which might very well have come within the province of the Board. Thus the Metropolitan Asylums Board was established in 1867 to deal with poor-law patients and to provide hospital accommodation for non-pauper residents, so that the Metropolitan Board was not the only central sanitary authority. The Board's position was still further weakened when in 1872 the Port of London sanitary authority was created under the control of the Corporation. Again, in 1870, another central authority was created under the Education Act—the London School Board. As the old chaotic system was being pulled down by the weight of its own disorder, Parliament was busy creating a new anarchy of *ad hoc* bodies, conflicting authorities and divided powers which is the characteristic of London's government to the present day.

As we have seen, the Metropolitan Board of Works represented a triumph of social necessity over political expediency. But in spite of its inherent defects the Board did carry through some vital improvements in the metropolis. Within ten years it had constructed a main drainage system for London—82 miles of main intersecting sewers connected to outfalls several miles away from the urban areas. The open sewers were filled in, and one of the most appalling dangers to London's health was removed. The Board also carried through the embanking of the north side of the Thames, and it freed ten of the Thames bridges from the obstructive tolls levied on passengers and transport. It acquired and maintained more than 30 parks and open spaces of about 2,600 acres, including such notable open spaces as Hampstead Heath, Clapham Common and Finsbury Park. Under the powers conferred under the Artisans and Labourers' Dwelling Act of 1875, the Board did some good work in clearing up a few of the worst London slums. Finally, it carried on a vigorous policy of giving London new highways, and was responsible for constructing several important thoroughfares, including Victoria Street, Shaftesbury Avenue and Charing Cross Road. The municipal dwarf had struggled manfully with some of the biggest problems in London.

At its worst, the Metropolitan Board of Works fully deserved the universal obloquy which was soon to drive it ignominiously from the scene ; at its best it cleared up some of the worst abuses, made a vital contribution to the health of the Metropolis, and showed what might be done by an effective central authority.

The system of indirect election based on the district boards and vestries was the fatal defect in the constitution of the Metropolitan Board of Works. The vestries had not sloughed off their worst faults under the new dispensation. They displayed the utmost apathy in carrying out their duties in the localities. Vegetable and animal refuse was left to rot in the streets for weeks. The majority of the boards and vestries completely ignored the new powers which were successfully entrusted to them for extending the public services in connection with public libraries, baths and wash-houses, the employment of crossing-sweepers, and the removal of nuisances.

" Vested interests in filth and dirt " were strongly represented on the district boards and vestries. Vigorous action could hardly be expected in respect of insanitary tenements when a large number of the vestrymen themselves were landlords of such tenements. Furthermore, the medical officers of the London vestries were often obstructed in their work. The vestrymen of St. James, Westminster, when they discovered that their medical officer took his work seriously, reduced his salary from £200 to £150 a year in order to discourage him. Dr. W. Farr, of the Registrar-General's office, told a Select Committee in 1866 that in certain London districts " the medical officer was under all sort of restraints. If he is active, they look on him with disfavour, and he is in great danger of being dismissed ".[1]

The Metropolitan Board, elected by these inefficient and corrupt local units, was bound sooner or later to draw into its constitution some of the flavour of corruption. Furthermore, the system of indirect election prevented the Board from securing any roots in the public imagination. It never came before the public to give any account of its work, or to seek the mandate of public confidence and support. It had the appearance of working in secret ; it governed, so it almost seemed, by a form of conspiracy, and in this atmosphere the rumours of jobbery and corruption were astir a long time before there was any solid foundation for the accusations. All this civic apathy in the capital was in very great contrast to the provincial towns where a vigorous municipal life was flourishing.

Once again the vigorous demand for municipal reform was heard in London. A League for Municipal Reform was formed by J. F. B. Firth, a London barrister, who was to give the rest of his life to the struggle to improve the local government of the metropolis. The demand was raised for one great unified system of government for

[1] Select Committee on Metropolitan Local Government (1866), Second Report.

London under a single authority, democratically elected, and possessing adequate powers.

In the last decades of the nineteenth century the Whig Governments were fairly sensitive to the pressure of public opinion, and a great unified system of government for London might have been secured—if the ancient and powerful barrier of the City had not stood firmly and implacably in the way. The City was not prepared to abate one iota of its ancient privileges. Even the most obvious minor reforms were successfully resisted. Sir John Grey, when he introduced a Bill for amalgamating the Metropolitan and City police forces had to admit that " whenever I touch any question which affects the alleged rights and privileges of the City, a power of resistance was shown, which it is difficult to estimate too high ".

It is perhaps unnecessary to add that the proposed reform of the police did not succeed, and that the square mile of the City remains protected by its separate police force up to the present day.

There is not space here to follow in any detail the struggle with the City for the municipal body and civic soul of London. The salient feature of that struggle was, briefly and simply, that the City always won. The Corporation successfully opposed reform measures which were introduced in 1858, 1863, 1868, 1869, 1870 and 1875. There was no mistaking the massive power and far-reaching influence which resided behind the gilded pageantry of the Guildhall.

The struggle culminated in Sir William Harcourt's Bill of 1884. His scheme was simply to extend the boundaries of the City and to divide London into municipal districts which would elect the Common Council, which in turn would elect the Lord Mayor. The ancient dignities of the City would be restored to a London, which, after long centuries, would once more possess a single central system of government.

The Bill would have preserved intact the ancient dignities of the City, and would indeed have based them on a structure as broad and solid as London itself. But the City obviously cared little for its ancient dignities. The City Corporations were concerned with more solid possessions than ancient dignities. An enquiry by a Royal Commission taken in the same year showed that the income of the Livery Companies alone was in the region of £800,000 a year in 1879 and the capital value of their property was about £5 millions. It is probable that their income today is about £2 millions a year and the value of their property at least £35 millions. It was obvious that the City had something worth defending. The City cared little for the mere trappings of power without its substance ; and the substance of its power was to be found in that rich square mile which Harcourt proposed to absorb into the commonalty of London. The Lord Mayor's hat was in the ring and the ermine-trimmed jackets were off.

The methods used by the City Corporation to defeat the Harcourt Bill were so openly scandalous that the Government was unable to resist the clamour for a Select Committee to investigate the charges. The investigations of the Select Committee showed that the ancient and dignified City of London, when its power was threatened, had no scruples about using methods which would make an American " party boss " look like a callow novice in political tactics. Tammany Hall itself had nothing on the gilded City of London when it got down to the bedrock of politics.

The Court of Common Council appointed a Special Committee to fight the threat of reform, and this Committee spent money on a lavish scale for the purpose of influencing Parliament by misrepresenting the state of public opinion, and for the intimidation by open violence of the supporters of reform. A great deal of money was spent in bribery and corruption of the crudest kind. The Special Committee of the City Corporation hired gangs of bullies as its "storm-troopers" and used them to break up the public meetings of the Municipal Reform League. It marched its storm-troopers through the streets in bogus demonstrations; it spent large sums in inserting notices of bogus resolutions in the Press, concocted reports of meetings, and forged counterfeit tickets in order to get its gangs of bullies into the meetings of the Municipal Reform League. It promoted a bogus organisation called the Metropolitan Ratepayers Protection Association to oppose the Bill and suppressed by violence any manifestations of dissent shown at their meetings. "This practice assumed proportions which could scarcely have been consistent with the public safety."[1] The ancient and dignified City had its mask off, and disclosed itself as an adept in thuggery, jobbery and public corruption.

The Lord Mayor himself exercised his right to sit in the House and lead the agitation against the Bill. Gladstone as Prime Minister spoke strongly in support of the measure.

The local government of London [he told the House of Commons] is, or if it is not, it certainly ought to be, the crown of all our local and municipal institutions. The principle of the unity of London has already been established under the pressure of necessity, as a matter which could not be resisted. It has been established in the Metropolitan Board of Works. . . . London, large as it is, is a natural unit—united by common features, united by common approximation, by

[1] Select Committee on London Corporation (Charges of Malversation, 1887).

common neighbourhood, by common dangers, depending on common supplies, having common wants and common conveniences. . . . Unity of government for the metropolis is the only method on which we can proceed for producing municipal reform.

But Harcourt's Bill never even reached the committee stage. Gladstone's Ministry was defeated in 1885 and was replaced by a Conservative administration under Lord Salisbury. Lord Salisbury was a staunch friend of the City, and a man with a very narrow outlook on the civic affairs of the capital city. He was later to undermine the authority of the London County Council on the grounds that London was not one great city but an aggregate of municipalities. The Harcourt Bill was quietly and effectively throttled by the Conservative majority. Once again, regardless of the consequences to the rest of the Metropolis, the City had triumphed.

Within three years of the defeat of the Harcourt Bill, however, the question of London's government was again forced to the front. We have already noticed the fatal defect in the constitution of the Metropolitan Board of Works which arose from its system of indirect election. The central body was increasingly infected with the corruption of some of its lower organs, the vestries and district boards, and at last its activities became so scandalous that the Government was compelled to order an enquiry. The results of this enquiry confirmed the worst accusations. Members of the Board and its staff were shown to be deeply implicated in a whole series of corrupt transactions relating to such projects as the London Pavilion, the sites of the Piccadilly Restaurant, Northumberland Avenue, and other public works in London. The corruption was so deep-rooted and so many prominent personalities were involved that it

"Vested Interests in Dirt and Disease" 25

became a matter of urgent political necessity to bury the Board of Works as swiftly as possible.

Once more, it had become essential to recast the government of London on the basis of a dire necessity. And once again, political expediency was called in to be the architect and draughtsman of London's government.

The Municipal Corporations Act of 1835 had laid the basis of municipal democracy in the provincial towns, but it had left the administration of the rural counties still in the hands of the justices of the peace appointed by the central government. By 1888, this ancient, inefficient and undemocratic method of county government could no longer be justified or even successfully maintained. The Local Government Act of 1888 let the breath of democracy into the ancient shires by providing the rural counties with elected councils in the place of the justices of the peace. In the process of introducing a necessary measure of reform in the rural districts, the great urban conglomeration of London was fitted abruptly into the form of the rural dispensation. The Metropolitan Board of Works was still in the process of being buried when the London County Council was thus ushered into its place by the backstairs.

It was in these circumstances that the present municipal government of London was created. Within six years yet another Royal Commission was to condemn the hasty makeshift of municipal government which had been conferred on the capital and to state that the problems of London's government were not solved by the Act of 1888. The vestries and the district boards were left virtually untouched. The Metropolitan Asylums Board, the London School Board, the Thames and Lee Conservancy Boards, the Boards of Guardians, the Metropolitan police force, and a large medley of smaller boards and numerous commissioners still retained their local government functions in the metropolis. The City Corporation remained in full possession of its territorial integrity and of its exclusive rights and privileges. In short, the municipal government of London was a body without a heart, an organism without control over its essential limbs.

The Act of 1888 has cast its long shadow over the development of municipal government in London right up to the present day. We shall encounter its consequences in many of the following pages. Here we can only note that possibly the most important of its consequences was that it made the proper organisation of London almost impossible to obtain since, by establishing powerful county councils in the Home Counties, it had thereby strengthened the resistance to any widening of the administrative boundaries. The development of London was pressed in upon itself. The problems of slum clearance and main drainage, to mention but two examples, were endlessly complicated and the living conditions of thousands of Londoners was depressed by the crippling restrictions on the capital's natural administrative development.

The boundaries of London today, with very minor modifications, are the same as those of the first Commissioners of Sewers in 1848. Those boundaries, in their turn, were based on the districts which compiled the old Bills of Mortality which gave the Court and Westminster an indication of the approach of the plague. When the present boundaries of London were fixed, almost a hundred years ago, barely two million people lived within those present boundaries. In 1939, four and a half million people lived in that same area, and another four and a half million people were living in the still Greater London which had grown up as an organic part

" Vested Interests in Dirt and Disease "

of the administrative county. The failures and stupidities, the obstructive tactics of the City and the deliberate neglect by Parliament had not halted the growth of London—but they had made it needlessly painful for millions of its citizens.

Chapter II
THE STRUGGLE FOR MUNICIPAL REFORMS

THE early Trade Union and Socialist movements had not played any large part in the development of local government in the Metropolis, or in the rest of the country.

The struggle for municipal reform was mainly carried on by Whigs and Radicals, sanitary reformers, merchants, manufacturers and all the stolid and expanding hierarchy of the middle classes who wanted freedom of trade, good drains and good value for the expenditure of public money. On the other hand, the appalling social conditions had driven the working classes in the early decades of the century into a turbulent struggle for emancipation. The town council and sanitary legislation did not bulk very large in the thoughts of men who were mainly concerned with the complete and, if necessary, violent transformation of society.

The birth of the London County Council, however, coincided with a formative period in the development of the British working-class movement. The great revolutionary surge of the first half of the century had subsided. The revolts and repressions of the " Hungry Forties " were a long way behind. The torchlight meetings, the insurrectionary plots, the riots and strikes of the Chartists were almost forgotten.

There were still, it is true, some echoes from those turbulent years. Hyndman, who had founded the Social Democratic Federation in 1881, was confidently predicting that 1889, the centenary of the French Revolution, would see the beginning of the " complete, international Social Revolution ". For Hyndman, the birth of the

London County Council was, no doubt, a very inconspicuous event. But it was none the less a great portent of things to come. The great majority of the British working-class had already made up their minds on the issue between revolution and reform. The way forward to Socialism, to the great and abundant society of the future, seemed to be through a policy of progressive social reform.

Many factors were responsible for steadily pushing working-class opinion in the direction of the evolutionary approach to political power. The British electorate had shown that they had no taste for revolutionary politics by decisively rejecting all the candidates of the Social Democratic Federation. Such majorities as 4,695 votes to 27, and 6,324 votes to 32 emphasised a plain lesson in electioneering tactics. And electioneering was coming steadily to the forefront as a subject of working-class discussion. The Reform Acts of 1867, 1884 and 1885 had widened the franchise and had redistributed the seats to give effect to the changed balance of the population. The opportunities for working-class representation in Parliament were greatly increased.

The Trade Unions were being remodelled by men whose aspirations were emphatically evolutionary. The defeats and failures of Chartism and Owenism had brought their recoil. The Trade Unions were moving strongly along the new and untried paths of prudence, financial stability and reasonableness. The Amalgamated Society of Carpenters and Joiners had actually written into its foundation charter that its members aspired to " become respectful and respected ".

This trend towards the acceptance of established ideas and institutions was strengthened by economic developments. The cost of living was falling steeply while at the same time money-wages were rising. Between 1873 and 1896 wholesale prices, measured by Sauerbeck's index, fell by 45 per cent. The purchasing power of the skilled worker in full employment was increased by about one-third. Under the influence of this steadily expanding standard of living, the powerful Trade Unions for skilled and semi-skilled workers were busy exorcising any spirit of strikes and unrest which remained in their ranks. The transformation of society by revolutionary action had ceased to be a real issue in working-class politics for a long time to come. The course seemed all set for reform by legislation.

The Fabian Society, formed in 1884, became the draughtsman of that legislation. It was the task of Fabians to give a concrete body of ideas to the existing tendencies. The Fabians were reformist and evolutionary. They abandoned such general principles as the abolition of the wage system and the right of the worker to the whole product of his labour. They were prepared to build upwards from the existing foundations. They began to formulate projects for social reforms which could be embodied in practical legislation. They regarded Parliament and the municipalities as the principal channels for social reform.

The Fabians were quick to recognise the opportunities for carrying out their projects which existed in the London County Council. They heralded the new Council's birth with No. 8 of their famous Tracts, *Facts for Londoners*. Sidney Webb was the author of this remarkable document which was described in the sub-title as an " Exhaustive collection of statistics and other facts relating to the Metropolis, with suggestions for reform on Socialist principles ". The pamphlet had all the great scope, accuracy and thoroughness which has characterised all the research of Sidney and Beatrice Webb. The pamphlet was packed with statistics which revealed London to Londoners. The facts had been dug out, one by one, from obscure and often unpublished sources. The ideas it contained were the raw material of Municipal Socialism, and they made a deep impression on the Progressives and the few Trade Unionists who formed the majority of the first Councils. It is perhaps no exaggeration to say that the new Fabian ideas first joined hands with the new Trade-Union principles on the floor of the London County Council. Both for London and for Labour it has been a fruitful and enduring partnership.

The new Council, elected in January 1889, reflected the forces which had struggled so long and so persistently for improved local government in London. J. F. B. Firth of the Municipal Reform League, and many others who had shared the long and bitter struggle with him, found places on that first Council. Sir John Lubbock, The Earl of Meath, G. W. E. Russell and John Benn were other men of outstanding ability who were returned at the first election. And, single portent of times to come, there was John Burns—" the socialist "—as contemporary newspapers were careful to label him. These men were all attracted to the Council because there was an immense amount of work to be done in all the main departments of local government, education, health, housing and the provision of all kinds of amenities. They called themselves " Progressives " and stood for the idea of one great municipal authority for London with increasing powers and a vigorous policy of social improvement.

On the other side was a small minority of Conservatives, who called themselves " Moderates ", and regarded municipal government as a negative affair, whose activities should be confined to utilitarian and financially unprofitable fields, and then only when the machinery of private enterprise had unaccountably broken down.

They were prepared to resist any extension of the Council's powers and activities, and their outlook was strongly dominated by the view that it is the primary duty of a Council to keep down the rates.

This cautious and negative attitude soon clashed with the crusading zeal of the Progressives. To some extent, the first skirmishes between the modern concept of private enterprise and the idea of social control of municipal and national resources were rehearsed on the floor of the London County Council.

Lord Rosebery was appointed Chairman of the new Council, and he brought dignity, competence and a broad tolerance to his task. His opening address to the first official meeting on 21st March, 1889, has, at this distance, a prophetic note as well as the ring of oratory.

If we proceed without prejudice and without affectation [he said], animated by a singleminded desire to do our best for London, we may live to elevate even this stupendous city; and the population which will come hereafter, unbounded and unborn, may look back with gratitude to this first Council endowed with powers which seem so great now and will seem then relatively so small—and recognise that in this cradle there lay a giant infant, the prophet and soul of a better dispensation that brought a new message of hope and prosperity to the people.

At the 1892 elections for the Council, Sidney Webb's pamphlet became the basis of the *London Programme*, which called, among other matters, for the complete municipal ownership of all the public utility services in London—gas, water, transport and electricity. In the hands of their private owners these services were inadequate and grossly inefficient, and the proposal to " municipalise " these utility services made an immediate appeal to the Progressives. It was the start of the Fabian permeation of the Progressive Party. At the

Struggle for Municipal Reforms 33

election Sidney Webb was returned at the head of the poll for Deptford, and together with five other Fabians took his place on the " Labour Bench " which formed a wing of the Progressive Party under the leadership of John Burns.

During the early years of the Council many other Trade Unionists, Fabians, and Socialists joined the new authority. Stewart Headlam, William Stephen Sanders, R. C. J. Ensor and J. Ramsay MacDonald were among the men and women of outstanding ability who took part in the early struggles for social reform in London. It is difficult to assess an individual contribution to a collective endeavour, but all those who have written about those days are unanimous in their tribute to Sidney Webb. His clear mind, with its infinite capacity for detail, was the guiding intelligence of many of the great reforms and improvements which were secured by the Progressives for London. It was, however, possibly in the field of education that Sidney Webb made his greatest contribution to social reform in the metropolis. He retired from his post in the Colonial Office in order to devote most of his time to the Council's work, and following his election in 1892, he was made Chairman of the " Technical Education Board ". Alderman Emil Davies has commented that Sidney Webb interpreted technical education as covering everything above elementary education, (which did not come under the control of the Council until 1904), except Greek and Theology and that during his eight years in the Chair he built up a " wonderful system of secondary education and placed university education within reach of the people of London ".[1]

Under Sidney Webb's guidance the expansion of the education services under the Council was steady and

[1] Alderman Emil Davies, *The London County Council* (1937), p. 8.

continuous. But it was not in this field that the first great battles of the early Council were fought.

During the years when London had lacked a common instrument of government, the great and small interests had been entrenching themselves at every point where they could levy their toll on the teeming population of the metropolis. These interests now arose up in all their formidable ranks to oppose the reforming spirit of the new County Council. There were thousands of landlords with profitable interest in the filth and disease of their slum tenements. There were the great owners of the London freeholds who would relentlessly oppose any restrictions on their freedom to exploit the land values created by the community. There were manufacturers who found it profitable to ignore the Factory Acts relating to the employment of children for excessive hours, and would resist any extension of the education services which would deprive them of their cheap and sweated labour. There were the vestrymen, many of them with their own private interest in slums and disease, who hated and feared the new authority and the reforming spirit which was its driving force. There were scores of public utility companies who plundered the consumers of the wealthiest city in Europe and gave them grossly inadequate and inefficient services in return for extortionate profits. These were the formidable cohorts of profit and privilege which, notably assisted by the ancient City, the Conservatives on the Council, and the deliberate obstruction of Parliament, were to involve London in the longest and bitterest struggle in the annals of local government in Britain. London had secured a common instrument of government, but there still remained the struggle to grasp that instrument and use it for the purpose of essential social reforms.

One of the first problems tackled by the Council was

Struggle for Municipal Reforms 35

public health. The Council had no direct control over the numerous sanitary authorities in the metropolis, but it promptly used its limited powers to appoint a Medical Officer of Health for the County, and began to investigate the causes of the numerous outbreaks of disease. In the previous chapter we have already seen how many of the vestries and district boards dismissed or reprimanded those of their medical officers who were active in carrying out their official duties. " The duties neglected by these vestries and district boards ", wrote Sidney Webb in the *London Programme*, " are more important than those they attempt to perform."

And now the London County Council was knocking at the door of this Augean stable of negligence and disease. The rallying of the opposition was immediate and powerful. The long struggle for the health and welfare of the citizens of London had begun.

The opposition became still more intense when the Council, at the suggestion of the Labour Bench, inserted a " fair wage clause " in all its contracts. The contractors met this attempt to prevent sweated wage conditions by promptly raising the price of their tenders, or by completely boycotting the Council's contracts. This procedure had an unexpected result. When the construction of the York Road sewer was under consideration, the Council's Chief Engineer estimated that the work could be done for £7,000. Only two tenders were received for the contract, both of them for more than £11,500. The Council thereupon took the obvious step of directing the Chief Engineer to carry out the work by employing direct labour. The sewer was finally completed for a cost of £5,163, apart from certain material costing £1,945, and several thousand pounds of the ratepayers' money had been saved.

As a result of this experience the Council decided to

set up its own Works Department, controlled by a special committee, to carry out such public works as the Council might decide to undertake without recourse to outside contractors. It was a project which would obviously result in substantial savings of the ratepayers' money. But a more important principle than the mere saving of the ratepayers' money was now at stake. Both inside and outside the Council there was a furious uproar at this attempt to remove some public work from the sphere of those private interests which had attempted to blackmail and boycott the Council into accepting their unfair labour conditions. The bitterness aroused among the Tory Moderates on the Council was so intense that for a long time they refused to serve on the Works Committee. They followed the contractors into a boycott of a department of their own Council. Time did not abate their rancour. A few years later they attempted to discredit the Works Department by bringing unfounded charges against its officers. One of the first acts of the Moderates when they came into power was to abolish the Works Department.

But it was the question of the municipal ownership of London's public utilities which aroused the longest and bitterest controversy. In recent times the Conservatives have been prepared to defend private enterprise on the grounds that it is cheaper and more efficient in its functioning than municipal or State ownership of the same resources. But at this period the Tories could not even allege the economy and efficiency of the public services which they were so ardently defending. Their defence was based simply on the naked principle of the " sacred right " of private enterprise to exploit its opportunities, regardless of the welfare of the community.

And in this question of London's public utility services the welfare of the community was very much at stake.

Struggle for Municipal Reforms

The private water companies, for example, were still carrying cholera, enteric fever and other water-borne diseases to the unfortunate inhabitants of the capital. A Royal Commission had reported in 1869 to the effect that the whole principle of the private ownership of London's water supplies was wrong, and that the grave dangers under company ownership could only be remedied by transferring the water supplies to public management. The Commission remarked that the duty of supplying the inhabitants of a city with water had been regarded as a municipal function from early times, and that the supersession of the municipalities by joint-stock companies was a modern innovation. " Of late years," they continued, " many towns in England have come to the conclusion that the new practise was a fundamental error ", and they had gone back to the old system of municipal ownership. With this tendency the Commission signified their full agreement. " A sufficiency of water supply is too important to all classes of the community to be made dependent on the profits of an association." [1]

But, with an utter disregard of consequence, the welfare of the community continued to be dependent on the profits of the water companies for nearly forty years. Commission after Commission was to tender the same urgent advice to the Government, without the slightest result. This deliberate neglect of the welfare of the people, this blunt refusal to apply any remedy to an urgent evil, almost baffles our credulity. The private water companies continued with impunity to pour a thin trickle of polluted water through their pipes. In the poorer districts one solitary tap, often fixed on the wall of a privy, had to meet the needs of a whole street or crowd of tenements. And then the water was only

[1] Royal Commission on Water Supply (1869).

turned on for a few hours a day, and not at all on Sundays!

The rate of charge for this dirty and scarce commodity was based on the annual rateable value of these premises. As a result, with every increase of house value in London the companies were able to raise their charges, without in any way increasing or improving their supplies. In fact, it was established in 1886 that the amount of water supplied daily to each house had been steadily decreasing over a period of ten years, but the water charges had none the less gone up by 80 per cent. The water companies were successfully holding the whole community to ransom, and at the same time they were carrying disease to every corner of the metropolis.

One of the first acts of the Council was the appointment of a Water Committee, which immediately approached the water companies to ascertain the terms on which they would dispose of their undertakings. The companies refused to treat on the issue, or to give up any control over their highly profitable undertakings. Unfortunately, there is not space to follow the long and fantastic struggle of the Council to acquire for London a water supply free from its dependence on profitability and pollution. The Council introduced a long series of Bills in the House of Commons to secure control of the water supplies of the metropolis. All of these Bills were either rejected by Parliament or allowed to lapse before they reached the committee stage. The long series of Conservative Governments refused to grant any new powers to the Council which would have enabled it to cope with one of the worst evils in London.

The water companies had their nominees inside the Council and in Parliament. Every string that could be pulled was pulled. The lobbying was persistent, powerful and successful. Sir John Benn complained bitterly that

Struggle for Municipal Reforms 39

the water policy of the Council was dominated by a chairman of one of the water companies. Eight Bills were introduced into Parliament in 1855 alone by the Council to acquire the companies undertakings, and not one of them reached the committee stage. The floor of the Commons was figuratively littered with the dead Water Bills of the London County Council. The grip of the water companies on the Government, and on London, was complete.

The Council's fight to secure a clean and adequate water supply for London lasted thirteen years. The water companies were sufficiently powerful to resist all attempts to oust them. Countless thousands of Londoners died from water-borne diseases, periodical epidemics swept the metropolis which medical officers and even Government Commissioners traced to the polluted supplies of the water companies, great fires ravaged buildings while the fire pumps were deprived of adequate water supplies, and year by year London was gripped by a " water famine " when the pipes yielded only turgid cupfuls of water.

After all these evils had gone unheeded for more than fifty years, when the danger to public health and the pressure of public opinion was overwhelming, the Government was moved to tardy and reluctant action. The Metropolitan Water Board was created, an indirectly elected body on the old and disastrously familiar pattern of local authorities in London. By 1902, some of the old anarchy of indirectly elected bodies with special powers had been swept away, but during the same period the Government, in its reluctance to concede any powers to the democratically elected government of London, was busy creating the new anarchy of still more powerful *ad hoc* bodies.

There is a financial footnote to this scandalous episode

in what Dr. Robson has called the "misgovernment of London". The companies received £43 million in cash for their undertakings. Since the capital monies spent by the companies in plant and equipment amounted in all to £23 million, the public had to pay the sum of £20 million to buy back the statutory rights and privileges which Parliament had conferred on the proprietors. The directors were also awarded £219,287 as compensation for their loss of office !

London is still paying a heavy price for the early mismanagement of its water supplies. The debt charges resulting from this vast obligation still consume 9*s*. in every £ of revenue received by the Metropolitan Water Board.

The other utility services in London were almost equally chaotic and extortionate in the hand of the unregulated private monopolies. The Tramways Act of 1870 had made the Metropolitan Board of Works the tramways authority for the administrative county, always excluding, of course, the City of London. The Board leased its concession to a number of private companies for twenty-one years, and these companies naturally selected the most profitable routes for their operations. Furthermore, under the Act the consent of the vestries was required before a tramways could be run through their areas, and one-third of the frontagers in a street could veto any proposal to establish a tramway in that street. The joint effects of private exploitation and public veto on the tramway system of London resulted in a chaotic system of unconnected services which bore little relation to the real needs and convenience of the travelling public.

When the London County Council was formed fourteen companies owned and operated about 107 miles of tramways in London. There was a complete lack of

Struggle for Municipal Reforms 41

any connection between these separate services and between them and the tramways beyond the County boundaries. A journey across London by the tramways in 1889 entailed frequent changes of tramcars and much hard walking in between. The fares charged by the companies were naturally as high as the public could be made to pay for transportation. This was an obvious field for municipal enterprise to establish the convenience of through and connecting services, with the economy of reducing operating costs and a considerable reduction in fares.

The Council had acquired the statutory right to purchase the tramway undertakings when their leases expired. The first of the leases effected was that of the London Street Tramways Company which operated about five and a quarter miles of tramways. The Progressives announced their intention of acquiring this undertaking when its lease expired in August 1892 as the first step to providing the metropolis with an adequate and convenient system of public transport.

The reaction to this proposal to provide London with an efficient transport service in place of the existing chaotic system was immediate and powerful. Once again all those interests which considered that their profits or their privileges might be threatened by the reforming spirit of the Council were united in compact and furious opposition. The Moderates inside the Council, when their debating powers were exhausted, adopted every possible tactic to obstruct, delay and prevent the Council acquiring the tramway undertakings. On two occasions when the question came before the Council, they walked out in a body to prevent an effective vote being taken, since the Statute required that two-thirds of the Council members must be present and vote on the issue. No effective decision could be reached in the face of this policy of deliberate obstruction, and the Progressives were compelled to lease the undertaking again, but this time for a much shorter period.

Once again we must add a financial footnote to an episode in the fight to bring the public utility services under municipal control. The London Street Tramways Company had claimed £604,000 for its short section of 5¼ miles. This grossly inflated claim for compensation was submitted to an arbitrator, who awarded the Company £64,540, and this reduction of nearly 90 per cent. was subsequently upheld on the Company taking its extortionate claim to the House of Lords.

It was not until seven years later that the Progressives were able to secure a sufficient majority in the Council to enable them to proceed with the task of providing London with an efficient system of public transport. Then the Conservatives in the Council and in Parliament went to every length in order to prevent the Council improving the convenience of the tramway services. The Metropolitan Boroughs, when they were formed, were given powers, which they fully used to sabotage the service by vetoing overhead wires. And, most extraordinary episode of all, when the Progressives attempted in the interest of elementary public convenience to join together the disconnected systems and to establish through services, every device of political obstruction was used to baffle the attempt. In order to join the tramway services, for example, on the north and south sides of the Thames the Council had to go to Parliament to secure the necessary powers. Six times in twelve years the Bills by which the Council sought to confer this obvious convenience on the travelling public were uncompromisingly rejected by Parliament. When the Council, after one of these rebuffs, decided to run a small omnibus between the two termini, the Council's power to under-

Struggle for Municipal Reforms 43

take this service was promptly challenged in the High Court. The Court of Appeal gave a decision against the Council. The omnibus service was stopped. The harassed and footsore public of London had to continue the weary trudge across Westminster Bridge to Charing Cross in order to get from one tramway system to the other.

We cannot follow the struggle for the public utility services in London any further in this brief account. There is no doubt that if the Progressives had won their fight London would have had cheaper, more comprehensive and more efficient public utility services than it actually had for a long time to come. Indeed London would have been a cleaner, healthier, better-housed, better-educated and better-planned city if the Progressives, Trade Unionists and Fabians had won the powers they fought for. But they did bring many far-reaching reforms to London, and even where they failed there is no doubt that they succeeded in considerably increasing the pace of reform.

There is one other comment which must be made here. The broader effects of the " gas and water socialism ", as it was called, of those Fabians and Progressives were profound and far-reaching. From the mustard seed of gas and water socialism has sprung the long series of Socialist proposals for socialisation on a national scale. The broad statement of general principles was narrowed down to a tight logical argument for the socialisation of each service or industry on its own merits. Those early struggles on the London County Council have left their deep imprint in the Socialist thought and practice of the present day.

These controversies on the London County Council had held the gaze of Britain. And London stood too much in the gaze of Britain and of the world for it to be a place where public ownership could demonstrate its efficiency. Birmingham could have its municipal savings bank, Sheffield its municipal gas and water, and Liverpool could run its municipal trams. But for the most obvious reasons a similar dispensation of social control could not be tolerated at the financial heart of Britain. All the forces of reaction were mobilised to bring the Progressive rule in London to an end.

In 1894 the Moderates declared their open allegiance to the Conservative Party, and sought the assistance of the powerful Tory national organisation in their electoral struggle to oust the Progressives. In November of the same year, Lord Salisbury, the Prime Minister and leader of the Conservative Party, made a violent attack on the London County Council at a meeting of the Conservative and Unionist Association. " We must not be shy ", he declared, " of using all our political power and machinery for the purpose of importing sound principles into the government of London." He went on to denounce the Council, " as the place where collectivist and socialist experiments are tried, and where a new revolutionary spirit finds its instruments and collects its arms ".

From that time onwards, the slum landlords, the vestrymen, the extortionate monopolies, and those other interests whose profits and privileges were threatened by the reforms of the Council, found that they had the open support of the Conservative majority in Parliament. The development of the London County Council was hindered and handicapped at every stage. Nearly all of its applications for the powers necessary to cope with the problems of a vast and rapidly expanding city were unceremoniously thrown out of Parliament. We have already seen with regard to water and transport that Parliament had set itself unflinchingly against granting the Council even those moderate powers which were necessary to carry out urgent improvements in the interests of public health or public convenience.

But this policy of mere obstruction was not sufficient. It was also necessary, in the view of the Conservative Parliament, to build enduring bulwarks against these " collectivist and socialist experiments " in public welfare and public enterprise. The Conservative Government, therefore, decided in 1899 to create, in place of the vestries and other local bodies, 28 rival authorities within the area of the County of London and to give them independent powers calculated to bring them into constant conflict with the London County Council. London had hardly acquired a competent central authority before its powers were to be undermined and its jurisdiction divided.

No one would dispute that the reform of the vestries was long overdue. Furthermore in a gigantic urban area like London it is hardly practicable to administer every local service through a single central authority, and some form of two-tier structure in local government is possibly essential. But the main purpose of the London Government Act of 1899 was not to create an efficient two-tier structure of administration. The Moderates jubilant attitude towards the Bill, Lord Salisbury's hostility to the Council and Parliament's deliberate policy of obstruction could leave few doubts as to the real purpose of the measure. The Bill had for its main purpose the undermining of the interest and authority which the Council had awakened in London.

Arthur Balfour's speech in Parliament when he introduced the Bill fully confirmed the fears of those who regarded the measure as an attack on the growing power of the London County Council. Mr. Balfour stated frankly that the Government did not intend to provide any co-ordinated link between these " new great municipalities" and the London County Council because any system of liaison, in the first place, " would inevitably drag these councils into the political vortex in which the London County Council appears to flourish ".

" Whose fault is that ? " shouted an indignant Liberal M.P.

Mr. Balfour continued suavely and imperturbably to lay the foundations of much civic conflict and division in the metropolis. " There is still," he went on, " another reason and a still stronger reason which guides me in this matter. I look forward to these municipal boroughs having a great and most legitimate influence with the London County Council. For these reasons we have not thought it desirable to introduce in this Bill any formal machinery for officially linking together the new municipalities and the London County Council."

The Government's intentions were made clear beyond doubt. In the words of one of the foremost critics of the Bill, " There was not to be one London, but thirty Birminghams."

Mr. Asquith was another bitter opponent of the Bill. He grasped the significance of the fact that the City was left untouched by the legislation, and declared it to be a scheme " to surround and buttress the unreformed City with a ring of sham municipalities to impair and destroy in most material particulars the corporate and administrative unity of London as a whole ". The unity of London, he went on to emphasise, was not only incomplete but impossible so long as the Government of the City was unreformed.

" When you call these new authorities municipalities," he declared, " you are giving them a false name. . . . What is a municipality as we here in England understand it ? A municipality is a community of spontaneous growth, self-governed and self-contained : a whole in

Struggle for Municipal Reforms

itself. There is only one community in the metropolis which answers that description, and that is London as a whole."

Thirty-six years after the passing of that Act, Herbert Morrison, from all his long experience of the London County Council and as mayor and councillor of Hackney —one of the boroughs created by the Act—pointed out again that the motive of the Salisbury Government was to overshadow the London County Council and to create jealousies between the London local authorities on the principle of divide and conquer. Mr. Morrison commented that there was certainly plenty of friction between County Hall and Town Halls, in which not only members but some officers had played their part.

To recognise the motives which lead to the creation of the Metropolitan Boroughs, however, is not to deny their great contributions to municipal improvements in London. But even the most civic-minded member of a Metropolitan Borough will usually admit that the improvements might have been secured far more easily, and that the pace of social reform in London would have been faster if the Boroughs had been created in the spirit of a team, instead of as twenty-eight individual challenges to the central government of London.

For a few years the eyes and aspirations of Londoners had been turned on their new central government at Spring Gardens. A sense of civic interest had been awakened after the long centuries of municipal confusion. A feeling of corporate vitality had quickened in the great mass of London. And then Londoners were suddenly asked to transfer their newly awakened allegiance to their local borough councils. In that abrupt divorce the ordinary Londoner was to lose a great deal of his civic sense for many a long year to come.

In local government London had become a city divided

against itself, a prisoner inside administrative boundaries which were forcing the density of population to insanitarily high levels, making the problem of town planning, slum clearance, drainage, transport and cleansing appallingly complex and difficult. A Government, which was not prepared to concede the necessary additional powers to the County Council, was proceeding to set up a new series of *ad hoc* bodies without any direct responsibility to the citizens of the metropolis. Apart from the water supplies and the tramways, the other public utility services were in the grip of private monopolies who were successfully holding the vast community of the metropolis to ransom. Such was the pattern of London's government at the beginning of the twentieth century.

The Progressives had lost their long fight to give London an efficient system of local government and to provide Londoners with good and cheap public services. But their record is not a catalogue of failures. They did much for London and for Londoners. When the Progressives had the powers they used them abundantly and well. They carried out great improvements in the London drainage system. They forced the reluctant vestries and district boards to carry out many of their neglected duties in public health and sanitation. They used their powers under the Housing of the Working Class Act, 1890, to clean up some of the worst slums in London; they checked some of the worst abuses of slum landlords, they carried out the great highways improvement scheme of Kingsway and Aldwych; they fought for and established the principle of betterment, whereby property owners could be charged a proportion of the increased value of their properties arising from public improvements.

Under the guise of technical education, the Progressives

Struggle for Municipal Reforms 49

created for London a far-reaching system of advanced education. Beginning where the legal powers of the School Boards ended, the Council, through its Technical Education Board, had in ten years laid down the lines of a highly complex system of specialised education, using the new polytechnics and its own technical institutes and art schools, which culminated in the technical faculties of the re-organised University of London.

Unfortunately, their zeal for educational reform was also to prove one of the factors which led to their downfall. Under the Balfour Act of 1902, the London School Boards and the denominational schools were brought under the administration of the London County Council. Many of the Progressives took a far from favourable view of the denominational schools which were being transferred to their care. The Council had no obligation to accept the transfer of a church school unless it was fit for its purpose. This raised an important issue. The question was whether the Council should give the denominations reasonable time to bring their schools up to date, or the law strictly interpreted and none but the fully efficient schools accepted. The tendency towards a strict interpretation was strengthened by the Nonconformists in the Progressive ranks who strongly objected to rate-aid for Church of England and Roman Catholic schools. On the other hand, a section of the Progressives took the view of Sidney Webb and the Fabians that the really important thing in the whole issue was that the Council should provide the best possible system of education for all the children under its charge.

It was a fateful dissension. Sidney Webb regretfully remarked that when the forces of religious conviction were aroused, electoral and financial considerations, the efficiency of the physical and mental training given to the children and even the continuance of any publicly organised and subsidised education at all, were as dust before the whirlwind. The Progressive Party on this issue began rapidly to lose the support of the clergymen, teachers and other sections of the community which had hitherto been enthusiastic supporters of their policy of reform.

The Tories were alert to grasp their opportunity. For the 1907 elections, the whole resources of the Conservative Party were mobilised to drive the Progressives from power in London. Their efforts in this campaign took on the quality of political desperation. For very good reasons. The Parliamentary election of 1906 had placed a huge Liberal majority in power in Westminster. The restricting hand of Salisbury was removed. The Parliamentary check on Progressive policies had disappeared. At all costs an alliance between a strong Radical Government at Westminster and a Progressive County Council had to be averted.

All the resources which the Conservatives possessed were thrown into the fight. The wildest extravagances of electioneering were used to stampede public opinion. Cartoons flooded the papers deriding the Council. The walls of London were plastered with posters showing a leering, greedy-faced lout labelled " Progressive Socialist Party " and below his outstretched fingers was the slogan " It's your money we want ". The wildest rumours were spread about the affairs of the Council and the fullest use was made of the religious issue.

With a thick-skinned indifference to political consistency the Moderates before the elections changed their name to the more attractive title of " Municipal Reformers ", thereby seeking to capitalise the popularity of the Municipal Reform League, whose policies of reform they had consistently opposed.

The internal dissentions among the Progressives, the

Struggle for Municipal Reforms

swing of public opinion on the religious issue, the high-powered publicity methods and the campaign of rumour and misrepresentation, had their results. The Progressives were beaten, and with an elected majority of forty, the " Municipal Reformers " held at last in their hands the power they were to wield in London for more than a quarter of a century.

The " Municipal Reformers " soon put into reverse the machinery which had been moving forward under Progressive impulses. They stopped the few municipal enterprises which were operated by the Council. They closed the Works Department. They tried to rid the Council of the tramways, but were compelled to desist by the pressure of public opinion. They neglected their responsibilities for the education of London's children so openly and flagrantly that the Board of Education withheld £10,000 in grant for their failure to re-organise the schools so that no class had more than sixty pupils !

We must pass swiftly over the period of Tory rule in London. It would be dishonest, however, to imply that the wheels of progress were totally stopped at County Hall during the long period of Tory rule. At the beginning, the Municipal Reform policy on the Council was bleakly simple—to carry out the statutory duties of the Council at the minimum possible cost to the rates. Their policy of retrenchment and rigid economy had its repressive effects on all the services of the Council. The worst of this phase, however, gradually spent itself. As the social consequences of this repressive policy were recognised by the more public-spirited members of the Municipal Reform Party, their influence was used to modify its results. Furthermore, public opinion could not be ignored, and the whole system of British society was sufficiently geared to policies of social and municipal reform to draw along the London Tories in its own momentum.

While it would be untrue, therefore, to suggest that the Municipal Reform Councils did not carry out important improvements in the services under their charge, one must with equal honesty admit that in most aspects of the Council's affairs the pace of reform was remarkably sluggish. The whole question of social progress, when shorn of its grandiose phrases, boils down to a simple equation in political dynamics. The Tories at County Hall, as at Westminster, had to balance their policy precariously between the demands of the public weal and the pressure of private interests. If they utterly neglected public interest, held up necessary reforms, and gave way too much and too openly to the pressure of the private interests, then public opinion would be aroused against them and their grasp of power would be endangered at the next election. On the other hand, their class interests and sympathies were intimately tied up with the landlords, the private manufacturers and monopolies whose very existence was threatened by every extension of Government or municipal enterprise. Conservative policy becomes an uneasy compromise between the actions of its left and right hands. Turning uneasily on this point of expediency, it is hardly surprising that, over many fields of local government in London, progress had to hobble forward on the uneven crutches of compromise and that there were other important fields over which no advance could be witnessed at all.

CHAPTER III

THE RISE OF THE LONDON LABOUR PARTY

THE failure of the Progressives gave rise to the demand for an independent Labour Party on the Council. The position as a subordinate wing of the Progressive Party no longer satisfied the growing aspirations of the Trade Union and Socialist movement in London. The "Labour Bench" was emerging from its municipal tutelage with clearer policies and a firmer cohesion than the Progressive Party had ever possessed. The transition from policy-making to party-making was easy and inevitable.

The London Trades Council, which since 1860 had exercised considerable influence on London's working-class movement, convened a conference at the Essex Hall on 23rd May 1914, to found a London Labour Party with the declared aim of securing independent Labour representation on the London County Council. John Stokes, the Chairman of the London Trades Council, presided over 338 delegates from Trade Unions and 86 from Socialist Societies. Fred Knee, the Secretary of the London Trades Council, moved the resolution "That this Conference . . . do constitute itself the first session of the London Labour Party."

This resolution was carried and the conference adjourned after instructing a Provisional Committee to draft a constitution. Charles Latham, later Lord Latham, was one of the members of this drafting committee.

The Conference reassembled in July 1914 and the draft constitution submitted by the Provisional Committee was adopted after some amendment. The London Labour Party was thus launched at a time when the world was standing on the threshold of the titanic events and vast changes of the First World War.

The early phases of that war were overshadowing most events when the first Conference of the London Labour Party was held on Saturday, 28th November 1914, and the first officers and the executive committee were elected. The first chairman was John Stokes of the London Trades Council, and the secretary was Fred Knee. Dr. Alfred Salter was elected treasurer—an office he held in unbroken succession until March 1942. The auditors were H. W. Inkpin and H. Stark.

The names of the Executive Committee will awaken many memories for the older members of the London Parties. The Trade Union Section consisted of Fred Bramley, Miss E. Cook, R. M. Gentry, Will Godfrey, G. A. Isaacs, J. Fineberg and Miss Mary MacArthur. The Local Labour Parties were represented by C. G. Ammon and the London Trades Council by Ben Cooper and F. A. Davies. The Local Trades Councils were represented by Councillor S. G. Weaver, the British Socialist Party by E. C. Fairchild, and the Independent Labour Party by James Mylles. The Fabian Society's representative was Miss A. Susan Lawrence and the Women's Organisations had Dr. Marion Phillips.

Fred Knee, the elected secretary, died before the end of his period of office, and on 27th April 1915 the Executive Committee decided to appoint a young applicant called Herbert Morrison as part-time secretary at the salary of £1 a week. It was to prove a fateful appointment for the youthful Herbert Morrison, and indeed for the London Labour Party itself.

The resources of the London Labour Party were very slender. There was a tremendous job of organisation to

Rise of the London Labour Party 55

be done. The young man with the unruly Cockney "quiff", the pugnacious jaw and the emphatic pointing finger found ample scope for his great resources of energy and organising capacity in the work of helping to create a political organisation which could cope with the immense tasks which so plainly lay ahead.

Labour in London certainly did not suffer from any political paralysis as the result of the "electoral truce" which had frozen the representation on the London County Council during the First World War. At the founding of the London Labour Party in 1914 the Party could claim the allegiance of only one member of the Council—Susan Lawrence. But in 1919, the Party stepped on to the stage of London politics with such energy and determination that it was promptly claimed as an ally by the Progressive Party, who suggested that the election should be fought in co-operation. The Labour Party, however, rejected the offer, holding firmly to the expressed principle of electoral independence of all other political parties.

In the 1919 election for the Council, the London Labour Party went to the polls with a comprehensive programme of municipal improvements and socialist reforms. The policies which had been developed inside the Progressive Party were reaffirmed. In a new political context the assault on the vested interests which had held up the social progress in London was renewed. The Labour Party repeated the demand for the municipal ownership of all the public services, including transport, fuel and food. Other items in the Labour programme called for the complete break-up of the Poor Law system in London along the lines laid down in the Webbs' famous Minority Report in 1909, and, as the latest heirs of the hundred years of struggle for effective municipal government in London, Labour demanded home rule for the metropolis in the form of a great municipal parliament with wide powers and the complete abolition of all the *ad hoc* bodies with the exception of the Borough Councils.

" Give Labour a Chance " was the appeal, and for a young untried Party the results of that appeal could be regarded with some satisfaction. Fifteen Labour councillors were elected and the Labour Party made its first appearance on the Council as an independent political party. Following that first wave of success, Herbert Morrison was appointed full-time Secretary of the London Labour Party.

We can follow only very briefly the succeeding steps in Labour's climb to power in London. At the 1922 election the London Labour Party increased its representation, including aldermen, to 20 members, on a programme which again called for public ownership of the public utilities, local government reform, slum clearance, town planning and radical steps for dealing with the London traffic position. The Labour Party on the Council now included Harry Snell, Susan Lawrence, Dr. Haden Guest, Cecil Manning, Emil Davies, C. G. Ammon, and C. J. Mathew, K.C., under the leadership of Harry Gosling of the Lightermans Union.

At the 1925 election the Municipal Reform Party still remained in control of the Council, but the progressive Party had dwindled to six members and three aldermen, while Labour with 35 elected members and four aldermen became the official opposition on the Council. Within nine years from that time the Labour Party was ready to move forward to take over complete control of the municipal government of the Metropolis.

The London Labour Party had not only taken the place of the Progressive Party, it had also assumed many of the same responsibilities, and it carried forward into

Rise of the London Labour Party 57

recent times the Progressive's fight for good public services and efficient local government in London. The patterns of its struggle were very similar in outline to those of the fight waged by the Progressives. The same interests were there to oppose and obstruct the pressure for reform. The slum landlords, large and small, were still to be found at the heart of any resistance to reform. The public utility companies were still holding London to ransom, only they had grown larger than their nineteenth-century predecessors and they were still more firmly entrenched in their positions.

One of Labour's longest and bitterest fights on the Council centred around the issue of London's transport services. In the previous chapter we have recorded the efforts of the Progressives to give the Metropolis an efficient tramway service. The coming of the petrol-driven omnibus brought a new problem to London's streets and a new opportunity for the private exploitation of yet another public service.

In the years immediately following the First World War, the various competing private companies in London's transport system were moving in the familiar direction of a public utility monopoly. This process was hastened by astute American financiers who provided the necessary capital for the proposed merging of interest. The District Railway and the Tube interests were amalgamated, and a controlling interest was acquired in the General Omnibus Company as a prelude to a policy of running off the streets or buying out all competing interests in the metropolitan transport. The next step brought the railway and bus interests under one managing board. One by one the other important transport concerns in London found their way into the all-embracing arms of the London Traffic Combine.

Almost the last vestiges of private competition were

removed in 1924, when the Government set up the London and Home Counties Traffic Advisory Commission with statutory powers to restrict the number of omnibus concerns which could ply for hire in London streets. This action amounted to the gift of a monopoly to the Combine. Within a short time the Combine was able to buy out almost all the remaining private concerns. The grip of the Combine on the vital arteries of London's transport would have been complete—if it had not been for the municipal tramways which the Progressives had acquired for London.

In these circumstances the municipal tramways became a factor of vital importance in providing the travelling public with protection against a policy of high fares. The tramways, by remaining outside the grip of the monopoly, prevented this policy from being carried out. Evidence of the influence of the tramways in forcing down the fares of the Combine could be found, for example, in the fact that where the tramways provided a twopenny midday fare the buses also reduced their fares to this amount—but only in the same areas which were served by the tramways.

The Combine now began a deliberate attempt to smash the municipal tramways of London. Omnibuses were concentrated on the tram routes at the most profitable periods in order to undermine the revenues of the tramway services. At the same time, inside and outside Parliament a tremendous amount of lobbying was done on the pretext of " traffic co-ordination in London ". A skilful press campaign was developed which represented the trams as standing in the way of the successful development of transport in London. Unified management of London's traffic was presented to the public as the cure for traffic congestion, faulty services, and every existing and imagined defect of the transportation system.

Even the London and Home Counties Traffic Advisory Committee, on which the Combine was represented, came out with a proposal on those lines.

In view of these facts it was with astonishment and alarm that those who were familiar with the true facts learned at the beginning of 1927 that private discussion had been going on for some months between representatives of the Combine and leading Tory members of the County Council. Later in the year the discussion became official, and it was announced that the Municipal Reformers proposed to transfer the management of London's municipal tramways to the London Traffic Combine.

The reaction of the London Labour Party was immediate. It was pointed out that the proposed transfer of the management meant the gift to the Combine of a still more complete monopoly of London's transport. The Labour Party reminded Londoners that the purpose of private management was not necessarily to provide public service but to secure the maximum possible private profit, and that the joint proposals of the Municipal Reformers and the Traffic Combine were highly dangerous to the travelling public of London. As an instance of the power of monopoly to exact enormous profits from the community, Labour pointed out that in 1927 no less than 3,719 million passenger journies were made in Greater London and that the increase of fares by even one-halfpenny would, therefore, mean an additional amount of £7,500,000 in the coffers of the Combine.

The London Traffic Co-ordination Bills were promoted jointly by the Municipal Reform majority on the Council and by the Traffic Combine. The Bills were strongly opposed by the London Labour Party, the Parliamentary Labour Party and the Labour Metropolitan Borough Councils, who joined together for the purpose of being legally represented in opposition to the Bills in the Parliamentary Committee. Attempts were made to rush the Bills through Parliament without success, and when the new Parliament elected in May 1929 met, the Bills still awaited their third reading in the House of Commons. But now a dramatic change had come over the scene. The Leader of the Opposition on the London County Council had become the Labour Minister of Transport. Strenuous efforts were made to persuade the Labour Government to reverse the position of the Labour Party on these Bills, but Herbert Morrison, as Minister of Transport in charge of the Bills, advised the House of Commons to reject them. The chance of a Labour Government had saved the travelling public of the metropolis from a complete monopoly of all their means of transport.

The problem of London's transport were dealt with in Herbert Morrison's Bill in 1931 which created the London Passenger Transport Board. All the means of transport in the greater London area eventually passed from private ownership into the control of a public corporation—the London Passenger Transport Board. The London Traffic Combine disappeared from the scene on the threshold of what had appeared to be its greatest victory.

The Labour Government in Parliament saved the travelling public of London from the exactions of a vast private monopoly in passenger transport. In the case of another vital public utility, electricity, this Parliamentary check was, unfortunately, not available.

The system under which London received its electricity supplies was chaotic and inefficient. In some districts the electricity supply was a municipal undertaking and in other districts the supply was in the hands of private companies. In the poorer districts of London the supply was carried on by the municipality, while in

Rise of the London Labour Party 61

the wealthier boroughs and outlying suburbs the supply was almost exclusively in the hands of private concerns. It is no exaggeration to say that in London the allocation of electricity supplies was based mainly on political considerations rather than on the technical basis of needs and efficiency.

Sir Harry Haward, for many years Comptroller of the London County Council, has described some of the consequences of this parcelling out of electricity supplies among a large number of minor concerns.

The current is alternating in some areas and direct in others; it was delivered at a number of different voltages, and is charged for under a bewildering variety of tariffs and rates with results that consumers living in one street are paying 3*d.* a unit while those in the next are charged 5*d.*, and electrical apparatus may become useless when the owner moves from one district to another. More than one company is often operating in the same borough.

Sir Harry Haward goes on to visualise the position which would have existed in London if the great schemes for a unified electricity supply which were prepared by the Progressives in 1905 and 1907 had been carried out. The waste and extravagance of the existing system was appalling. Millions of pounds had been spent in equipping redundant generating and distributing plant for no less than seventy-seven separate stations.

An opportunity to redeem the years of waste and inefficiency was presented by the legislation which gave the London County Council power to acquire the private electricity undertakings in the Metropolis in 1931. But the manifesto and appeals for funds of the Municipal Reform Party had frequently carried the signatures of men prominently connected with the privately owned electricity companies. This was another instance where private interests might be allowed to triumph over considerations of cheapness, efficiency and public convenience. This alert expectation may have lessened the surprise, but not the indignation, when in 1924 it was learned that the Tory Council was proposing to postpone the purchase of the private companies from 1931 to 1971, thereby extending for another forty years the wasteful and expensive system of generating and distributing electricity in the London area.

The Labour Party on the Council was plunged into another long and bitter struggle to prevent an extravagant and extortionate system being foisted on the metropolis for another forty years. The fight was carried from the Council into Parliament with the promotion of the London No. 1 and London No. 2 Electricity Bills, which postponed the purchase date to 1971 and set up a scale of prices and dividends which were exceedingly generous to the companies. Dividends were sanctioned at 10 per cent. until 1931 and at 7 per cent. thereafter, together with ingenious additions, which meant in effect that a much higher rate of dividend than 7 per cent. would be secured within a relatively short time.

Labour lost its long fight in the Council and in Parliament, and within a very short time electricity consumers in the company districts of London were noticing the effects of the legislation. Company prices were much higher than those obtaining in the neighbouring areas where there was a municipal undertaking. In the years before the war, a constant series of complaints were being made about the high prices charged by the private companies. Water, gas and electricity in London have testified forcefully to the waste and inefficiency of private enterprise.

It is not possible to follow in any further detail the rise of the London Labour Party to political power in the metropolis. The attention of the Party was by no means

Rise of the London Labour Party 63

exclusively focussed on the London County Council, important though that sphere of activity was in itself. There were all the manifold problems of creating the effective political and electoral machinery for assisting the Local Parties in Borough Council elections, with elections to the Boards of Guardians, and the sixty-one London constituencies which returned members of Parliament. Furthermore, year by year, the development of the vast urban conglomeration of London thrust up some new political, social or economic problem for the London Labour Party to grapple with. There was a continuous demand on the thoughts and energies of all who served Labour in London during the years of planning and organising before 1934. And the final electoral success was to bring even heavier burdens and responsibilities.

Each year the annual estimates of the Council gave Labour an opportunity of challenging Municipal Reform policies over the whole range of the Council's services. On many of these occasions the vigour of the Labour Party's attack on some important issues of public policy had prolonged the sittings of the Council long past midnight, and on one occasion almost until noon of the following day.

Year by year the Labour Party on the Council sought to obtain a more effective policy for dealing with the urgent questions of overcrowding and slum clearance in the metropolis. And again when the Council was moved to tardy action on these questions, the Labour Party strongly opposed the proposal to deal with the urgent question of rehousing by erecting inferior types of tenements which would rapidly have degenerated into new slums within a very short time.

In the field of the education services, the Labour Party tried hard to secure many more open-air schools and secondary schools, extensive improvements in the buildings and accommodation at the existing schools, and much wider opportunities for technical and advanced education.

The Local Government Act of 1929 which transferred the duties of the Boards of Guardians and the hospitals of the Metropolitan Asylums Board to the Council, presented the opportunity, as the Labour Councillors pointed out, to break up the repressive Poor Law system in London, to introduce much more socially effective methods of dealing with the problems of human destitution, and for building up through the transferred hospitals one of the most comprehensive municipal services in the world.

Most of these suggestions were ignored, and the Council's administration of Public Assistance in London was to prove so harsh and inhuman that it stirred all sections of London opinion to angry protests, and became an important factor in the downfall of the Municipal Reform Party at the next election. The Labour Party also strongly opposed the " economy cuts " which were imposed on the whole range of the Council's services in 1930-1, pointing out that economies in the social services, apart from even the grievous hardship they inflicted on thousands of children and sick and unemployed people, were defeating their own aims by restricting the field of employment and thereby increasing the existing depressed conditions.

We shall deal at greater lengths with some of these conflicts in the following chapters. It would be wrong, however, to convey the impression that the two main Parties on the Council worked in conditions of unending conflict. We have looked at some of the matters on which they were sharply divided. But the members of a local authority cannot always live in the fierce atmosphere of party politics. A great deal of the work of any Council is concerned with the solid and painstaking

Rise of the London Labour Party

details of administration. The Council chamber is the sounding-board of party differences. But behind the floor of the Council, away from the eyes and ears of the public, in hundreds of committees, much of the real solid work of the Council was done. Political differences tend to disappear when, say, the Education Committee is considering the plans for a new school, or a Hospital Committee the design for a new style of hospital bed. In these circumstances the most acute political differences can be submerged in a public-spirited desire to reach a decision which will best serve the needs of that particular school or hospital and its pupils or patients. While, therefore, political differences occupy the centre of public attention, it is as well that those other sides of the functioning of a local authority should not be forgotten.

The same sense of public responsibility which contributed to the work of the committee-room also characterised the Labour Party's attitude on the points of division and conflict. Harry Gosling, Emil Davies, and the other early leaders of the Labour Party on the Council, had laid it down as an inflexible principle that Labour in opposition should always aim at putting forward proposals which were sound in themselves and capable of being carried out should the Party become responsible for the conduct of the affairs of the Council. This tenet of political consistency was taken up by Herbert Morrison when he became leader of the Opposition on the Council ; he continually emphasised that it was morally wrong and politically injurious to urge policies in opposition which could not, or would not, be implemented when in power.

These, then, are but a few of the influences and conflicts, the personalities and policies, which gathered around and helped to shape the London Labour Party in its rise to power. And that power was not long denied to it. At the 1934 election, London returned 69 Labour

Councillors out of a total of 124. On the basis of this representation Labour became entitled to 11 aldermen, and the final balance of the parties in the Council, therefore became, Labour 80, Municipal Reform 64. The government of the largest city in the world had passed into the hands of the Labour Party.

At the following election in 1937, Labour increased its representation to 75 councillors and 12 aldermen. It was an election which was strongly reminiscent of the Conservative effort to drive the Progressives from power in 1907. Once again the whole resources of the Conservative Central Office were flung into the fight, and once again a Tory Prime Minister brought the influence of Westminster to bear on the affairs of the County Hall. With a few notable exceptions, the majority of the local and national newspapers opened their columns to a flood of misrepresentation and distortion. The expenditure on all forms of publicity was lavish. The Municipal Reformers even imported the Transatlantic device of the telephone canvass and over 300,000 London subscribers were rung up and urged to support the Tory candidates. A "last word" from the Prime Minister was sent to every elector.

In an interview with the *Manchester Guardian*, Herbert Morrison made the following comments on the election :

All the varied and not too scrupulous resources of the National Conservative machine—Mr. Baldwin, Sir John Simon and the Government; all the interests—West End Hotel proprietors, Stock Exchange people, the landlords, and others, who did not come to the surface ; the whole Tory press, the Communists, who so elaborately played the Tory game, and the Fascists—we have beaten the lot. This is more than a party victory, more than a Labour victory ; it is a victory for decency in politics and for the constitutional principles on which British public administration is assumed to be founded.

Rise of the London Labour Party 67

A large number of Liberals have contributed to the result. Nay, more, a considerable number of Conservatives who admire our constructive work at County Hall, and who became increasingly disgusted with the depths to which the campaign against us descended, voted for our candidates.

The Government let it be known that they wanted to decide what kind of a County Council our citizens should choose. It was another of the long line of attempts to turn the capital into a crown colony.

A Conservative Prime Minister, the City, the landlords, the interests which did not come to the surface, the attitude which sought to treat the capital as a crown colony ! These were the interests which had sought to restrict the growth of popular influence in London during many centuries of its long history. Times have changed, London itself had changed, but at the heart of all opposition to social progress there still remained the familiar and formidable concentration of property and privilege.

Chapter IV

THE GOVERNMENT OF LONDON

In 1934 London had a population and a revenue greater than that of many European states.

In fact, it is true to say that the Government of a small European state had a much less arduous and complicated task than that of grappling with all the manifold problems and difficulties of Britain's capital. Herbert Morrison, with an intimate experience of both central and local government, has indeed inclined to the view that in direct executive administration County Hall has a bigger job in peacetime than the British Government itself.[1]

In the previous pages we have seen something of the process of neglect and obstruction which has given London a system of local government different from that of any large urban area in Great Britain. London has to tackle the problem of the greatest city in the world with a machinery of self-government less adapted to its functions than that of a smaller English borough. That is the anomaly, and the grave handicap, of municipal government in the metropolis.

This poorly adapted machinery of local government is the background against which the achievements of the local authorities in the metropolis must be judged. There is also another aspect of local government, in London and elsewhere in Britain, which must always be taken into account in estimating the quality and results of municipal achievements—the regulating influence of the Central Government itself.

Under the Weimar Republic the big cities of Germany,

[1] Herbert Morrison, *How London is Governed*, p. 41.

like the so-called " Free Cities " of the United States, possessed wide powers to raise their local revenues and to spend them as they thought fit for the benefit of their inhabitants. The position is very different in Great Britain, where legislative authority is required for even the most trifling expenditure of public money. It is not possible for any local authority in Great Britain to set out to create a grand municipal Utopia for its inhabitants. The local authority must function within a rigid system of judicial and governmental controls. Furthermore, the District Auditor, with his wide powers of surcharge, is the alert sentinel of the system who can bring swift financial retribution to any body of councillors who have strayed a fraction beyond the defined limits of local government expenditure.

The controlling hand of the appropriate government department is felt in every section of a local authority's activities, although the method of control varies with the different types of municipal activity. In some cases the control is exercised over the appointment of officers of the Council ; in other instances it takes the form of making the grants for the various local services conditional on their conforming to certain requirements ; or, again, the form of control may be simple and direct with the prescription of duties and their enforcement, if necessary, by legal penalties.

It is within this complicated framework of controls, restrictions and injunctions that a local authority must work out its policy of administration, levy its rates, and decide how it can best serve the welfare of its citizens. In the circumstances, it might be imagined that the views of the majority on the council was a matter of small consequence since municipal action is circumscribed by such a prickly hedge of restrictive legislation. But this system of controls does not result in municipal uniformity, as anyone who has an opportunity of comparing the quality of the services provided by similar types of local authority in this country is well aware. The outlook of the majority of the councillors determines the policy of the council, and that policy can reflect itself in sound administration, better social services, the setting up of other services which have been neglected because of the permissive or optional character of the legislation under which they are promoted, and the provision of a whole series of local improvements and amenities. Without in any way imposing undue burdens on the ratepayers, the local council can make an enormous contribution to the health, happiness and welfare of the local inhabitants.

It was within the rigid limits of this legislative framework that the Labour majority at County Hall had to implement their vast programme of slum clearance and rehousing, Public Assistance reforms, improved educational and hospital services, new welfare services, better recreational facilities, and a large number of other reforms and improvements which were regarded as necessary for the welfare and happiness of Londoners. It has, however, been necessary to dwell on the limitations of local government because there were some political enthusiasts who imagined that with the advent of a Labour majority at County Hall the millennium had descended on London or, at least, that the London Labour Party would immediately proceed to implement a " bold socialist policy " in every sphere of London's life and labour. It was obviously not so simple as all that. There were many reforms in London which can only be carried out when a Labour majority at County Hall receives the sanction of a Labour majority at Westminster.

It was not within the power of the London County Council, for example, to revise completely the scales of relief payable under the Public Assistance regulations.

But they were able to ensure that the regulations were far more generously interpreted in favour of the applicants, they could ensure that the whole system of relief administration was suffused with a new humane spirit, and they could enormously improve the standards of accommodation and diet in the various institutions under the Council's charge. They could press forward, step by step, securing at each stage the necessary sanction of the Ministry of Health, so that by 1939 the last vestiges of the old repressive system of Public Assistance in London had been merged in the new concept and new system of Social Welfare.

The London County Council could not, without the sanction of the Board of Education, increase at its discretion the number of teachers in the Council's schools, or completely abolish the payment of fees in all London secondary schools. But the Labour majority could considerably improve the existing education facilities and provide much wider opportunities for advanced and technical education for a lot more children and adults in London. They could use to the fullest extent the existing powers of local authorities to provide better medical, dental and welfare services in the schools. They could bring forward their projects for a large number of open-air and secondary schools and, on the basis of proven needs, secure the approval of the Board of Education for their erection.

They could not " nationalise " the land of London, but they could use their compulsory powers to acquire the sites and tear down vast acres of slums, build thousands of new homes, and take steps to girdle London with a great " Green Belt " for the health and recreation of the citizens of the metropolis and of the counties far beyond the metropolitan boundaries.

Sufficient has been said to show the opportunities, as

well as the limitations, on progressive municipal policies in London. The long era of Municipal Reform administration, with its generally repressive effects on social and municipal improvements, had created wide and generous opportunities for progressive policies in London. But there was no swift road to reform in London. The structure of London's government imposed its own limitations, the magnitude of the metropolitan scale of things added to its complexity, and even the enabling legislation presented a more formidable barrier than was the case with any other authority in Great Britain.

We can only make a passing reference to the complex mass of Acts, Statutory Orders and departmental regulations, which define, guide and control almost every phase of local government activity in London. The metropolis is largely governed by special London Acts relating to Building, Public Health, Finance and other local government activities. The Local Government Act of 1933, which consolidated and amended the law relating to the constitution and administrative functions of the other local authorities in the country, did not apply to the London County Council and the Metropolitan Boroughs. It was not until 1939 that a similar consolidating Act was passed for London—the London Government Act, 1939.

The aim of much of this legislation is to bring the exercise of local government functions in London under the direct scrutiny of Parliament, and in consequence the activities of the Council have been singled out by Conservative majorities for special discrimination to an extent which was not possible in the case of any other local authority in Britain. There are many eyes in Westminster which still stare suspiciously across the river for signs of those " socialist and collectivist experiments " which so agitated Lord Salisbury.

The Government of London

Another serious difficulty arises from the enormous variations in the rateable value per head of the London Boroughs on which the Council issues precepts to obtain its Funds. For example, a rate of a penny in the £ before the war produced £46,181 in Westminster and £3,112 in Poplar. Yet the dense population of Poplar obviously required more extensive social and public services than the residents of Westminster. The machinery for equalising the burden of rates was, and remains, very unequitable. The City, " that small island of obstinate medieval structure in the midst of a sea of modern local authorities ", the richest square mile in the world, where the produce of a penny rate yielded over £34,000, managed its own finances and remained the lowest rated area in the administrative county. In 1938 the City Corporation spent over £9,000 in banquets and receptions alone—the product of a threepenny rate in the Borough of Stepney.

These are a few of the factors—legislative, structural, financial—which have a direct bearing on municipal policies in London. They fix the channels along which those policies must move, and, on occasions, they can regulate or halt the pace of reform.

These difficulties and defects, however, do not cast their reflection into the machinery of the Council itself. As a piece of democratic machinery, the London County Council can stand comparison with any local authority in the world. The Council is probably unique among local authorities in the recognition which it extends to the Opposition on the Council. The position of Leader of the Opposition, as well as Leader of the Council, derive official standing from the practice and Standing Orders of the Council. The safeguards which protect the expression of minority opinions are numerous and extensive. Members of the Council may place on the agenda for debate notices of motions regarding any matter which affects any aspect of the Council's work, or relating to the welfare of the people of London. Further safeguards of the rights of minorities are provided, for example, that on the formal proposal and seconding any matter may be referred to the appropriate committee of the Council for consideration and report, and this report may become the subject of debate in the Council chamber. Moreover, at each public sitting of the Council an opportunity to ventilate points about current administration is provided by putting questions to the Leader of the Council and to the chairman of committees. If the questioner should regard the reply as unsatisfactory he can move the adjournment of the Council, and after a five-minute speech, a formal seconding, and a five minutes' reply, ten members can force a division of the Council.

The standing of the Opposition on the Council is further recognised by the provision that party representation on the main committees and sub-committees is in proportion to the party strength in the Council. Finally, the Opposition itself is recognised in the presiding dais of the Council, the Deputy Chairman being appointed by the Opposition. In short, the Council is so ordered that the democratic regulation of an effective Opposition can be brought to bear on all aspects of administration.

The position of Leader of the Council is one of heavy responsibility. His real task is to organise and co-ordinate the work of the majority party, deal with all the difficult questions which may come up on the committees, or arise from Parliamentary or other causes, and generally to keep a careful control over all the main developments of administration and policy. It is no exaggeration to say that the position of Leader of the London County

The Government of London

Council is the most difficult and arduous position in the whole realm of British civic administration. Writing in 1935, Herbert Morrison stated that he had

> already found that the responsibilities of a Leader of the Council who takes his job seriously are as heavy as those of a Cabinet Minister with a busy Department, although the salary of the Leader of the Council is nothing, and that of a Cabinet Minister is between £2,000 and £5,000 a year.[1]

The organisation of the Labour Party on the Council is designed to correspond to the framework of the Council. In the first place, there is the organisation of the Labour Councillors throughout the various committees of the Council. The Labour members of the hospital, education and public assistance committees, for example, have a group meeting before each meeting of the full committee.

The Policy Committee of the Labour Party on the Council consists of the Chairmen of the main committees and the Party Whips. In peacetime, it meets every week and affords the necessary opportunity for taking a comprehensive view of all the phases of the Council's work and for deciding general matters of policy. The decisions of the Policy Committee are subject to the approval of the Party meeting which is held before each Council meeting. It might be claimed that this closely knit system of Party organisation has succeeded in reconciling two political incompatibilities since it successfully combines energetic leadership with the process of democratic control.

The First Chairman of the Council, Lord Rosebery, laid down two important objectives for members of the Council at its inaugural meeting—" real hard work and the abstinence from oratory ". The abstinence from oratory has certainly remained a conspicuous feature of

[1] Herbert Morrison, *How Greater London is Governed*, p. 78.

the Council chamber. Members cannot speak for more than fifteen minutes without consent of the Council. When that time limit has expired, the Chairman informs the Council accordingly, and unless the Council signifies its agreement to hear him further the member must sit down. This simple device has shorn speeches in the Council of most of the ornamental aspects of oratory. Members learn to speak simply, factually, and very much to the point.

As for Lord Rosebery's first injunction—real hard work —every conscientious member of the Council gets plenty of it. The Council meets at 2.30 on Tuesday afternoon and the Agenda, Minutes and Reports of the meeting may sometimes run to as many as a hundred closely printed foolscap pages. These reports often deal with highly complex matters, and no member can discharge his duties unless he, or she, is prepared to undertake a lot of real hard work in reading up and mastering a mass of detail. In addition to the Council meetings, every councillor is expected to serve on two or more of the main standing committees and sub-committees which usually meet weekly or fortnightly. Then there are other sub-committees to attend, Council institutions to inspect, and committees of management of hospitals, schools and mental institutions on which a member must serve ; public meetings to attend, and the regular meetings of Party organisation at which the member must be present ; and, not least in importance, there are the needs and problems of his own constituency to be considered. The position of a councillor on the London County Council is obviously no sinecure. And the work and responsibilities of a chairman or vice-chairman are even still more heavy. In short, a member of the Council must be prepared to devote a large proportion of the working week to the affairs of the Council.

The Government of London

Since all this public service is done without any material regard, it is obvious that we have here touched upon a serious problem in democratic representation. The number of people who can afford to give this amount of time to the affairs of the Council is comparatively few, and the members of the Council must accordingly be drawn from a limited circle. This is not the place to discuss the implications which arise from these circumstances, or to debate the question of payment of councillors. It is, however, certainly a question which must be faced in any proposals for the reform of local government not only in London but also in the case of the County Councils and some of the County Boroughs in this country. Here we can only record that, so far as the London County Council is concerned, the amount of time required from councillors has tended to confine Labour's representation to people with independent means, to those whose income was derived from occupations which did not depend on normal working hours, and to trade union officials and married women.

It is necessary to record this position. But it would certainly be impossible to claim that London might have been better served if the Labour councillors had been drawn from a broader section of the community. In view of the achievements recorded in the following pages, it is difficult to see how the vast work of municipal reform might have been better carried out than by the men and women who had the responsibility during the first decade of Labour's rule in London. That much stated, let it also be said that the present Labour councillors are themselves concerned about the problem of ensuring that the contribution to London's government should be shared by the broadest possible cross-section of the metropolitan community.

Below the immediate level of the Council chamber,

however, and even around its very portals are the channels where the full tide of London's democracy can come sweeping in. As if to correct a certain exclusiveness in its inner circle, the Council summons up a vast army of public-spirited men and women from every rank of life to share the tasks of civic administration at nearly all the levels where the Council's services touch the lives of the people of London. Before the war, there were no less than 1,500 committees and sub-committees of the Council with over 14,000 places. The total number of councillors and aldermen is only 144, so a great army of Londoners are drawn intimately in to the working of the Council.

The score of Standing Committees of the Council are the pinnacles of a vast hierarchy of committees and sub-committees on which various powers and duties of the Council have been conferred. The extent and actual working of this great system of " delegated administration " are too complex to be adequately discussed in this section. A brief outline of the committee system which covers the Education Services will convey a general impression of the system.

The Education Committee of the Council is composed of fifty members, of whom thirty-eight are members of the Council and twelve are co-opted by reason of their special knowledge or experience in the field of education. This committee deals with the broad issues of policy relating to the whole field of education in London, and it must accordingly delegate certain powers and duties to sub-committees which cover specialised aspects of education. There are seven sub-committees to which certain powers and duties of the main committee are distributed—Elementary Education, Higher Education, Special Services, Books and Apparatus, Staff Appeals, General Purposes, and Teaching. Already the co-opted

The Government of London

membership of these committees is large. The doors of these committees are by no means closed on the ordinary citizen of London, but there is a tendency to confine their membership to men and women who possess some detailed knowledge and experience in the respective fields of the committees' work. That is the superstructure of the Education Committee system; below this level it broadens out very rapidly to cover the whole working of the education services.

The co-opted element on the committees now becomes so large that the official core of councillors and aldermen are almost lost to view in the broad mass of their fellow citizens surrounding them at the committee tables. The Elementary Schools, both provided and non-provided, are grouped so that each three or four schools come under statutory bodies called School Managers. The co-opted members of these School Management Committees are drawn from every walk of London's life. One of the Council's divisional officers acts as clerk to the committee, and it must be emphasised that the duties and powers of the School Managers are by no means formal or perfunctory. The influence of a good body of school managers can be felt in every aspect of the school's administration. Furthermore, the committee work of the members is supplemented by visits of inspection to the schools under their charge, which brings them into direct contact with the problems of school administration and enables them to keep a check on the decisions which have previously been made in committee.

Similarly, Governing Bodies are appointed for the county Secondary Schools and Training Colleges, and Advisory Committees for the Technical Schools and Schools of Art. Managing Committees are also appointed for each residential, open-air, nursery, approved schools and homes. Finally, and not least important, are the School Care Committees composed of voluntary workers who interest themselves in the general welfare of the children, advise parents how to obtain suitable medical treatment for their children, and assess charges to parents for school meals and for children maintained in residential open-air schools.

We have now traced a system under which several thousand men and women are drawn in a purely voluntary capacity into the work of administering the education services. There are obviously certain important consequences of this system. At every stage the work of the paid official comes beneath the scrutiny of people who possess a certain public-spirited outlook and an interest in the school, nursery or home under their charge. A powerful check is thus established on what are called " bureaucratic tendencies ". Furthermore, these committees become, as it were, the sensitive attenae of the main committee above them, keeping them informed in a real and practical way of what is happening in the schools and services at every level of administration. The Education Committee is able to react quickly to those changes in the social and economic life of the metropolis which are swiftly projected into the lives of hundreds of thousands of children. During the decade of the Labour majority on the Council, there have been many improvements and reforms in the education services introduced in the Council chamber which were inaugurated in response to information and suggestions which came up the channel of committees from the men and women who were, so to speak, working on the spot.

Similar structures of committees and sub-committees cover the other main services of the Council, including the Hospital and Medical Services, Social Welfare and Mental Hospitals.

The results of this vast leavening of the Council's work by the principle of co-option has not received the attention it merits from those who are concerned with the problem of the democratic control of large units, both local and national, which are becoming the prominent feature of current trends and theories. There can be no serious reservations, however, about the way the committee system functioned under the Labour majority at County Hall, right up to the outbreak of war. With the notable exception of Public Assistance—which we will consider later—the committee system of the London County Council became an instrument which increased the effectiveness and the quality of the Council's achievements. There were two factors which undoubtedly contributed to making this vast committee system into an effective instrument of municipal progress.

In the first place, the Labour Party is an organisation which can be made very sensitive to the impulse and promptings of public opinion. There was, then, on the part of the Labour councillors a readiness to consider and to act on the flow of information, suggestions and criticism which was piped back through committee channels. In turn, the members of the various committees right through the length of the system, knew that their recommendations were being considered, and, where necessary, promptly acted upon. The whole system became immeasurably more alert and sensitive.

Secondly, the quality of all the committees was greatly improved by the general tendency of the Labour Party to make appointments to the committees on the basis of the individual capacity and experience, instead of as part of a system of political patronage. Herbert Morrison laid it down as a general principle that " co-opted persons should be so selected as to add to the quality of the committee concerned. Co-option should not be regarded purely as a means of adding to the strength of the parties, or merely of conferring an honour."

It was an idea which in practice worked extremely well. There was many a solid Tory member of a local hospital committee, who, while uncompromisingly rejecting the idea of a State Medical Service, none the less worked with unremitting enthusiasm to secure the best possible amenities and equipment for the municipal hospital under his care !

CHAPTER V

CLEARING AWAY THE SLUMS

BEFORE the war Greater London was acquiring more than 80,000 new citizens every year. The London area had become a centrifugal force of immense power, drawing in population and industry from the whole of the British Isles.

This immense process of expansion was utterly without guidance or plan. The Government made no attempt to control the migration of industry into the London area, although it had reached an extent which was dislocating the balance of industry in the whole of the country and making the revival of the distressed areas far more difficult to attain. Inside the London Area, the London County Council and the other local authorities had no adequate powers to guide or control the vast surge of new building. The last available open spaces inside the county were swallowed up and the factories and houses began to sprawl out far into the countryside. There was nothing to guide or restrain the devastating onrush of the speculative builders.

This vast, planless growth of the metropolis raised immense social and sanitary problems. Factories were built in residential districts, without regard to the amenities, increasing the pressure on the existing housing accommodation and turning homes into overcrowded warrens. Industries sprang up in the countryside and the speculative builders rushed up an inchoate huddle of new houses in the vicinity, without regard for the provision of schools, libraries and other social amenities, creating problems for the local authorities which were almost insoluble. The roads leading out into the countryside were swiftly beaded with the " ribbon development " housing of those who wanted to escape from it all. But the attractions of the country amenities they sought were soon swallowed up in a new onrush of building.

Land values soared, rents climbed, and the pressure of the poorer sections of the population on the existing housing accommodation became still more intense. Under this pressure whole acres of dwellings were breaking down into slums every year. The new slums grew ; the old slums festered ; and very little was done about it all.

That is a brief outline of the problem of housing and of town planning which confronted the Labour majority on the London County Council in March 1934. But before we deal with the way these immense problems were tackled, let us look at them a bit closer. Let us try to get them into perspective in terms of the Londoners who lived in the crowded tenements and squalid slums of this great imperial city.

Houses have always been hard to get in London if you earned less than £5 a week. More than half the population in London had to live in multiple occupation—which means that 750,000 families in London had to share their front-door key with another family. The standards of a few of these multiple tenancies were very comfortable indeed. Large Victorian houses converted into dignified and spacious flats. And let at dignified rents !

But for the great majority of Londoners multiple occupation meant no structural division between their domestic life and that of their neighbour. It meant sharing the same bathroom—when there was one. It meant stumbling over the neighbour's pram in the hall. It meant hearing the bawls of the neighbour's baby and being compelled to listen to the neighbour's radio set.

Clearing Away the Slums 85

At the best it meant the loss of that domestic privacy which is the essential quality of a home. At the worst it meant something far below the level at which life begins to be civilised and tolerable at all.

In fact, living conditions were a long way below that level for a very great number of Londoners. The Census returns and the various reports of the local Medical Officers of Health give us a vivid glimpse into the cramped, squalid and teeming dwellings in the metropolis in the years before the war.

Over 1,500,000 people, comprising 313,000 families, had a standard of accommodation of more than three people to two rooms. That figure was bad enough. But when we begin to analyse it a bit further we get some idea of the appalling living conditions in London. More than 500,000 people had a standard of two persons to one room, and 47,305 people lived at a greater density than four people to a room. 16,251 people lived, cooked, ate and slept at a density of more than five people to a room. And there were tenements, mews, cottages and basements where the pressure of human beings on the available living space was more than six, seven, eight, nine and even more than ten persons to a single room.

This was London. This was the centre of the civilised world—the greatest city on earth. A primitive native from an African kraal, considered unfit for the responsibilities of self-government, might well have recoiled in horror from the dense squalor of a tenement in the great imperial city itself.

The problem was not a localised one. The East End did not possess the monopoly of slums and overcrowding. It is true that conditions were very bad in the eastern boroughs of London—Stepney, for example, had a population of 250,000. The average size of a Stepney family was four persons and the average accommodation for that family was three rooms. Another quarter of a million people lived in even worse conditions in Shoreditch, Finsbury and Bethnal Green. But the blight of insanitary living conditions spread far beyond the confines of the East End. The Royal Borough of Kensington, for example, had as many as 13,000 insanitary dwellings. In Southwark over 40,000 people were living in appallingly overcrowded and squalid conditions. The Medical Officer for Southwark describes cottages which had no yards, no back windows, no water taps. In this same borough there were at least fifty instances of two-roomed cottages holding families of ten or more people.

Battersea, Bermondsey, Hackney, Paddington, Greenwich—in each of these London boroughs there was the same situation of human beings forced into squalid and insanitary proximity. Time and the distended tenancies worked their grim delapidations with the buildings. But you have to delve a bit deeper into the official reports to find out what was happening to the people's lives.

The following table speaks with startling emphasis of the incidence of death and disease in four of the densely crowded boroughs of the metropolis as compared with four of the least densely populated districts. Lewisham, Hampstead, Wandsworth and Woolwich are by no means ideal municipalities so far as housing is concerned. In all four there are insanitary areas which exercise their concealed influence in pushing up the rates of mortality and disease. But their densely housed population is much lower than that of Bermondsey, Finsbury, Shoreditch and Southwark. I have extracted the figures from the Registrar-General's Statistical Reviews. The figures for population density shown in the first column are the densities of population per acre of land, including open spaces and inland water.

Clearing Away the Slums

	Population Density	Death-Rate	Infant Mortality		Death-Rate		
			Under 1	Under 2	Respiratory Tuberculosis	Pneumonia	Bronchitis
Lewisham . .	31	10·1	49	6·9	0·73	0·71	0·69
Hampstead .	39	11·4	55	7·1	0·56	0·70	0·59
Wandsworth .	38	11·1	58	7·0	0·81	0·67	0·66
Woolwich . .	17	10·8	53	5·9	1·09	0·67	0·76
Bermondsey .	74	14·0	77	10·3	1·25	1·63	0·91
Finsbury . .	119	14·7	72	10·4	1·31	1·34	1·47
Shoreditch .	147	14·2	85	14·9	1·23	1·54	1·20
Southwark . .	151	14·3	74	11·9	1·15	1·39	1·15

Note : The death-rates are in respect of period 1921–30 and are based on rate per 1,000 living.

There is no need to stress the significance of these figures. And they tell only a part of the story. Rheumatic heart disease, kidney complaints, influenza, the notifiable diseases, levy a far higher toll in the densely crowded boroughs of the metropolis. And there are other physical consequences of bad housing conditions which are not reflected in the mortality tables—rheumatism and arthritis, defective hearing, poor eyesight, septic tonsils and stunted bodies were some of the penalties which thousands of children and adults had to pay for living in the crowded and insanitary tenements, mews and underground basements of the metropolis. Medical authorities have estimated that if we could reduce the overcrowding in our great cities to the very modest level of three people to two rooms there would be an annual saving of the lives of 15,750 children and 33,000 people at later ages. We bury 48,000 victims of bad housing every year.

The foregoing is a brief indication of the immense problems in health and housing which confronted the Labour majority in 1934. The position of slum clearance and re-housing in London was falling a long way behind most of the provincial towns and cities. Even the worst provincial cities kept in check the areas of slums and overcrowding. In London alone the insanitary areas were spreading fast and far, like a corrupt fungoid growth moving across the face of the metropolis.

The long succession of Tory Councils had barely touched the problem of London's slums. The chief part of the Council's housing activity had been on several large housing estates outside the County boundary, the largest being at Becontree, St. Hilier, Downham and Watling. These housing estates added to the fringe development of London, but they left the growing slum areas inside the County largely untouched. The rents on these housing estates were usually far beyond the means of the slum dwellers. Furthermore, the estates had been developed without proper regard to local employment and the daily fares back to their places of work inside the County usually put these " country cottages " beyond the reach of the people for whom they were ostensibly intended. The vast areas of slums inside London remained intact. Year by year living conditions· became more squalid and wretched for thousands of Londoners. Year by year the pressure of population on the available dwelling-space increased. Year by year whole acres of London property were sinking down to the slum level.

This failure to clear up the vast insanitary areas of the metropolis was arousing increasing public concern. The persistent pressure of the Labour Party and the reports of the medical officers and social investigators were making slum clearance an issue of major public importance. At each triennial election for the Council the Municipal Reform Party produced a comprehensive slum clearance and housing programme. Unfortunately these programmes were seldom fully carried out.

In July 1933 Herbert Morrison revealed the great gap between the election programme and the actual achievements of the Council. In 1919 the Municipal Reform Council proclaimed its intention of building 29,000 houses in five years as London's share of the " homes fit for heroes " ideal. The heroes actually got 375 houses in five years. The second proclamation of 6,000 houses became 2,055 houses. Under the Wheatley Act of 1924 the programme promised 20,000 houses, but less than 12,000 houses had emerged three years later. The grandiose programme of 1930 was translated into bricks and mortar to the extent of 118 houses in four years.

In proportion to the needs of the metropolis, the housing performance of London was a long way behind that of most provincial cities. By 1930, Birmingham, with one-fifth of London's population, had built as many working-class houses as the metropolis. Despite the fact that in London building costs were from 15 to 20 per cent. more than in other parts of the country, the cost of working-class housing in London was equal to 1·094d. rate. Included in this rate was the loss under the 1919 Housing Act which was fixed at the produce of a penny rate. It would appear, therefore, that the rest of the post-war housing in London by 1930 was borne by a rate of 0·094d. In Birmingham the cost falling on the rates for the same period was 6d. in the pound.

If the housing performance bore little relation to the urgent needs of London, the actual pace of slum clearance was even more disproportionate to the immense requirements. The total housing schemes of the Council over twenty years were insufficient to house even the 100,000 Londoners who had to live in 30,000 underground basements which had been condemned as unfit for human occupation. And the basement dwellers were only a part of the total insanitarily housed population of the metropolis. In Finsbury 24 per cent. of the families in the borough occupied one room ; in Shoreditch 23 per cent. ; in St. Pancras, 22·6 per cent. ; in Holborn, 22·3 per cent.

In the light of these requirements the pace of slum clearance was appallingly slow. Here is an example of the progress of a slum-clearance scheme. The local authorities, under the Housing Acts, were given notice in 1904 to clear a slum in Bethnal Green housing 1,800 people. The Council replied that the clearance could be safely " left to private enterprise ". In 1913 the slum was still there and the authority said that they were anticipating helpful legislation. In 1914 the Government held an enquiry into the slum ; in 1915 it ordered the London County Council to carry out the clearing. In 1922 the work was begun ; in 1930 the slum had been rebuilt. In a quarter of a century one small slum was swept away. Such was the tempo and spirit with which the slums were tackled in London.

There were experts who, knowing the difficulties which were attached to London's slums and overcrowding, would have advised the Labour majority to deal cautiously and progressively—meaning slowly—with the problem. This was not the Labour view. With Lewis Silkin, M.P., as chairman and C. W. Gibson as vice-chairman, the Council's Housing and Public Health Committee faced their enormous task with a determination to press on swiftly with the job. The Committee set to work on the basis that the campaign for the clearance of the slums was to be conducted with continuous vigour until every London slum had gone.

The first step was to clear the larger areas of slums so

that sites could be secured for rehousing. In 1934 the Council adopted a programme for clearing 132 acres of these large sites, affecting over 80,000 people. The ultimate aim of the programme was to clear the existing areas of slums within a period of ten years, and at the same time to take adequate steps to deal with the serious overcrowding in many London boroughs. This time the Council had adopted something more than a mere paper programme. There was both the determination and the energy to tackle this stupendous task.

The first step was to create the organisation for this immense undertaking. This first step might have been swifter and easier to make. But in 1931 the majority of the May Committee had advocated the " economy axe " as the single infallible method of promoting prosperity and saving our financial integrity. And the Tory Council, following faithfully on the heels of its big brother at Westminster, had used its own small axe with considerable vigour. Among the places where the axe had lopped vigorously had been the housing departments of the Council. In 1934 the efficiency of these departments was still impaired. Architects, valuers and all the other technical staff had to be engaged and the departments supplied with all that was required in skill and materials.

The plans were prepared, the staff and equipment mobilised. The areas were selected for clearance and the legal procedure was set in motion. Now, except for the specialised legal mind, the tortuous ways of the law are dull and dreary by-ways for the more simple-minded citizen. But the legal procedure by which a local authority before the war acquired the power to clean up the dens of misery and disease in our great cities is worth looking into—particularly at a time when the rebuilding of Britain's blitzed cities is in the forefront of discussion.

Under the then existing housing legislation there were two methods open to a local authority to deal with what the Housing Acts describe as " the rehabilitation of an insanitary area ". The Council could proceed either by (1) a Compulsory Purchase Order, or (2) by means of a Clearance Order. The initial procedure in both cases is to some extent similar, for it is the duty of the local authority to secure the clearance of the area and to provide for the rehousing of the people displaced. The main difference between the two methods is that under the Compulsory Purchase Order the local authority acquires the property, demolishes the buildings and itself redevelops or disposes of the site. Under a Clearance Order, however, the site is left in possession of the owners, who are required to demolish the insanitary buildings themselves. It is perhaps significant that in the great majority of cases the Labour Council decided to use the compulsory powers of purchase, itself pulling down the slum property and becoming solely responsible for the standard and type of new dwellings which were erected on the site.

Let us follow the procedure a little further. The Housing Committee selected the area to be cleared ; the Council's Medical Officer of Health, the valuer and the architect submitted their separate and detailed reports on the area—its population, the rents paid, the estimated cost of the acquisition and the provision for the necessary rehousing accommodation.

After consideration of these reports by the Housing Committee, and after any special points had been disposed of, the proposals were submitted to the Council. The Council approved the scheme and made the formal declaration required by the Housing Acts. The Council's valuer could then proceed to make a list of all the owners and lessees of property in the area. The time taken

Clearing Away the Slums

over this detail depended to a considerable extent on the readiness with which the information was supplied. It was the first stage at which the reluctance and obstruction of the property owners could begin to operate, and on many occasions six or nine months was spent in securing and confirming all the necessary information regarding the property owners in the area.

The Medical Officer of Health also prepared his own detailed evidence of the insanitary conditions of the area for the information of any possible objectors to the clearance scheme. The next requirement was for the Council to make public its intentions by advertising the scheme in the Press.

We now pass on to a higher level. The scheme was submitted to the Minister of Health and given preliminary consideration by him. If there were any objections which had not been withdrawn a public inquiry had to be held. This inquiry usually took place in the town hall of the Borough in which the property was situated, and was conducted by an inspector of the Ministry of Health. The Council and the objectors were both usually represented by counsel. Expert witnesses appeared for both sides. After the inquiry the Ministry's officer made an inspection of the area, and in due course the Council was informed whether the scheme was approved, together with any modifications thought necessary by the Ministry.

The confirmed scheme was again advertised, and a period of six weeks had to elapse in order to give any person who was dissatisfied with the public inquiry an opportunity to apply to the High Court before the Council could exercise any of its powers.

If the Council was proceeding by a Clearance Order under which the landlords retained the site and looked after its redevelopment themselves, then those powers were swiftly exercised. The Council merely served notice on the owners requiring them to demolish the insanitary dwellings within a specified period. The Council found the tenants new homes, and the lawyers would pick up their briefs and depart.

On the other hand, if the Council intended to acquire and redevelop the site, instead of leaving it to the landlords, there was still a great deal of work for the lawyers to do. In this case the next step was for the Council to send formal notice to the landlords in the area of its intention to acquire the property, and request them to submit their claims for compensation.

Now it is undoubtedly true that slum property is one of the safest and most remunerative forms of capital investment. A yearly income of £300 from an eight-room house in a London slum was by no means unusual. Houses which let at £70 a year were often sub-let at rentals of £250. One house in South London with seventeen rooms was let to twelve families, numbering 72 people, at rents from 16s. to £1 8s. a week, and that was no exceptional instance. It is obvious that in these circumstances the slum landlord will rate the site-value of his property very highly indeed. The Council's valuer must then begin negotiations to obtain a more reasonable basis for the payment of compensation. If after protracted negotiations the purchase price could not be agreed, then the dispute must be referred to arbitration under the Acquisition of Land (Assessment of Compensation) Act, 1919. An independent official arbitrator conducted the inquiry, and, once again, the lawyers and the expert witnesses made their appearance and expressed their firm and conflicting opinions. In due course, the arbitrator's award was published and became enforceable. The rest of the proceedings were completed by the usual formalities associated with the transfer of real property.

Clearing Away the Slums

At last, the council was able to do something about knocking down the slum.

That brief outline will convey some idea of the legal complexities which awaited the Labour Council in connection with each clearance area. This legal procedure often swallowed up from eighteen months to two years of valuable time while it followed its exacting and predetermined course. That was under favourable circumstances. But circumstances were not always so favourable.

From the beginning, the Labour Council's attempt to clear up the London slums had met with bitter and unrelenting opposition from large numbers of slum landlords. The intricate procedure laid down by the Housing Acts, with its elaborate provision for protracted negotiations, public inquiries and appeals to arbitration and the High Court, provided ample cover for those landlords, who were determined to fight a stubborn rearguard action against the Council's approach to their insanitary dwellings and the unfortunate people who were compelled to live in them. In some cases two hundred or even more landlords were involved in a single clearance scheme. The determined opposition of a single landlord could enforce the whole of the protracted procedure outlined in the previous pages, and could hold up the effective clearance of the area until the public inquiries and arbitrations had yielded their tardy results.

But the landlords were not the only people who could summon the long delays of the law to their assistance. There were many others who had strongly-rooted interests in the poverty and squalor of their slums. There were, for example, tradesmen who protested that their sources of income and profit would disappear with the slums. There were a score of private interests which could be summoned up by slum clearance notice to jostle and plead to retain their vested interests in human misery, dirt and disease. The Labour Council soon discovered that there were indeed some formidable locks to the social prison-houses which constituted the London slums.

Finally, lest it be thought that I have been unduly prejudiced in my description of the legal requirements which relate to slum clearance, let me record the informed comments of the three eminent lawyers and the two distinguished surveyors who presented the Uthwatt Report :

> The preparations and bringing into operation (of a slum clearance scheme) is necessarily a lengthy task under a system based on negotiation with existing interests, and, although time limits are imposed by Statute for the completion of each stage, the Act enables the period to be extended. In practice it usually takes several years for a scheme to reach final form. Moreover, even when the scheme is operative, the planning authority has only limited powers to compel or hasten development or redevelopment. A critic might be forgiven for thinking planning was regarded as a sin or a luxurious pleasure, not a duty.

We have glanced at the tangle of legal procedure, but we have still to count the cost. Let us turn back to the slum itself, back to the people who may not even have been aware that an elaborate and costly process of the law had been concerning itself with their fate. The last verdict has been given, the final assignment of the title deeds has been signed, sealed and delivered to the Council. The time has come to begin moving the people out of the slum.

It is at this point that the Housing Committee began to come up against the hard core of the slum problem in London. People could not be decanted out of even slum dwellings until other accommodation was available for them. Furthermore, this alternative accommodation

Clearing Away the Slums

had to be made available at rents which the people who were being rehoused could afford to pay, and that accommodation had to be reasonably close to their existing places of work so that their means were not strained by heavy travelling expenses. Essentially, it boiled down to the same problem on different scales for both the Council and the slum dwellers—how much money was available to secure the new dwellings which were the only alternative to the existing slums.

As we have seen, London was an intensely overcrowded city, the denser the population, the higher the land values, and the higher the land values the more difficult it becomes to deal with slums and overcrowding. The only people who could afford to smile at this social conundrum were the landlords, who could sit back and watch the value of their properties soaring as the result of the activities and discomforts of the rest of the community.

Before the war, site values in London had reached fabulous limits. Sir Charles Bressy, the planning expert, estimated that the cost of an insignificant street widening in central London worked out at the rate of £2,000,000 a mile. The cost of land for housing in Bermondsey was about £22,000 an acre; in Lambeth £29,000; in Holborn £45,000; Finsbury £37,000; Stepney, £33,000 and Westminster £48,000. It was obvious that at these rates slum clearance, redevelopment and town planning in London had indeed become what the Uthwatt Report described as expensive luxuries.

As we have seen, no practical solution could be found in moving the people out of the slums into the surrounding counties where land was cheaper to acquire. The hard crust of built-up land was already stretching out fifteen or twenty miles from Charing Cross. The vast majority of slum dwellers could not afford the daily fares back to their places of work. Furthermore, the transport services in London were already burdened to the utmost limit with the daily insurge and outflow of more than a million people who lived outside but worked inside the County boundaries. If a few hundred thousand daily travellers were added to that total the means of transport would become choked even beyond the endurance of the wretchedly overcrowded inhabitants of London's slums.

It was obvious that, within the finances and powers possessed by the Council, the problem of London's slums had to be tackled and solved at the place where they had arisen. There was no other practical alternative which would enable the slums to be dealt with at all.

The complicated pattern of difficulties presented by each slum area had to be examined in detail and its individual solution discovered. In one district, for example, the site of a jam factory became available through the amalgamation of two companies. The factory site covered an area of $5\frac{3}{4}$ acres, and on this site it was possible to erect nine blocks of modern flats with 1,104 rooms. A few hundred slum dwellers in a neighbouring area were moved into these new flats and their own insanitary dwellings were pulled down. This opened up a new site, which in turn would enable another area of slums to be cleared.

In another borough the Council acquired one of those old houses with a couple of acres of grounds which had stubbornly retained its seclusion in the midst of a densely populated area. A hundred families found new and modern homes on this site, and their dark tenements were pulled down to provide the opportunity for a new housing scheme which, in turn, enabled another insanitary district to be cleared.

The rehousing of thousands of Londoners thus became a series of complicated moves in which the squares of the

Clearing Away the Slums

chess board were represented by acres of buildings. But the people were never treated as the simple pawns of these vast transactions. The human side of each transfer was never neglected. Before any move was made, before even the property was acquired, the Council had complete details regarding every man, woman and child in the area—their places of work, the rents they paid, the number in each family and other relevant details. This information formed the basis of what may be called the social strategy of slum clearance. The placing of the tenants, for example, was based on their family requirements, families with children being provided with flats on the lower floors, and the requirements of old people were also especially kept in view. The actual arrangements for the removal were carried out by a staff of women assistants specially trained for this work.

There was some need for this skilled and sympathetic assistance. The change from the cramped squalor of a slum to the relative spaciousness of a brand-new dwelling, freshly decorated and fitted with modern conveniences, called for some degree of adjustment on the part of the people concerned. Many of these slum dwellers, adult men and women, had spent their whole lives in the crowded hovels and tenements which the Labour Council was sweeping away. For the great majority of their children the narrow alleyways, the crowded streets, the vermin infested and mildewed room had been their only playgrounds and homes. Many of these women had hardly had a kitchen sink of their own, let alone modern cookers and proper household facilities. And now for the first time there was living-space in the home. There were the modern facilities of gas or electric cookers, there were baths, airing cupboards, and walls which reflected colour instead of the drab patterns of grime and dampness. For most of them it must have been like coming out of a long dark tunnel and suddenly finding themselves surrounded with space, sunlight and clean breathing air.

The difficulties of sites, finance and legal procedure were not the least of the problems which the Labour Council had to contend with as their programme of slum clearance got under way. As their programme gathered momentum it began to stir up an insidious campaign of calumny and slander about the people Labour was trying to move out of the slums. There is no doubt that this campaign was inspired not only by slum landlords who were apprehensive about their investments, but also to some extent by certain political circles who became apprehensive that Labour might succeed where others had neither the will nor the courage to venture. " Sensational stories " about slum dwellers began to appear in the columns of certain sections of the local and national Press. Special investigators touted around the slums in search of " revealing disclosures ". There was talk of slum minds, slum habits and slum diseases. This campaign was not without its effect in certain quarters. There were " overspill " areas which strongly opposed the housing of slum tenants in their districts. There was even one comfortable Borough which fought hard to prevent a home for aged horses being pulled down in order to furnish homes for human beings.

As long ago as 1866 John Ruskin and Octavia Hill had demonstrated by providing slum dwellers with decent homes that slum habits, where they exist, were the results of slum environment. The Labour Council, seventy years later, found an equal readiness on the part of London's slum dwellers to respond to the changed environment. The Council's officers on the new housing estates did not find any of the proverbial cases of coals being kept in the bath. They found that very few people indeed were so badly warped that they preferred dirt to

Clearing Away the Slums

cleanliness. Instead, they found an almost instant response to the higher standards of the new environment. They discovered a universal eagerness to make the utmost use of all the modern conveniences with which the new dwellings had been fitted. They discovered a vast thankfulness for the new opportunity for decent living conditions which had so unexpectedly come the way of their tenants.

We have followed this complicated business of rehousing London's slum population through a maze of difficulties. I have sketched the vast accumulation of neglect, the inadequate organisation for tackling the job, the slow and tortuous patterns of legal procedure, the complications involved in the transfer of large numbers of people, the stubborn resistance of slum landlords and others with vested interests in the slums, and, finally, the attempts of certain political opponents to obstruct and delay the rehousing of London's citizens. It all adds up to a fantastic catalogue of difficulties. In the circumstances, what has been written might well seem to be the apology for a failure instead of the prologue to one of the biggest achievements in municipal housing in London, or indeed in any other city in the world.

Let us take a look around London four years after Labour had come into power at County Hall.

London, in peacetime, was used to watching gangs of workmen tearing up the streets for repairs. But peacetime London was certainly not accustomed to seeing whole acres of buildings being torn down in the poorer districts and new buildings going up swiftly on the old sites. In April 1938—four years after the Labour Council got to work—there were extensive demolitions and building operations going on in nearly every borough in London.

In Hammersmith the vast White City site of $45\frac{1}{2}$ acres was being cleared and prepared for the erection of several thousand modern dwellings and a well-planned shopping centre. In Wandsworth, on a site of 25 acres, blocks of modern flats were swiftly arising on the foundation of an old insanitary area. On the Rockingham Estate in Southwark an area of 17 acres had been redeveloped to provide modern dwellings in place of the dark insanitary tenements which had been huddled on this site. In the Phoebe Street area of Poplar and Stepney 10 acres of the worst slums in Britain were being wiped out. Ten acres of hovels in the Dove Row area of Shoreditch were prepared for demolition. On the King's Mead Estate of 20 acres over 500 new dwellings had been created and another 500 were on the way. At Woodbury Down, Stoke Newington, the freehold of a 74-acre site had been acquired on the banks of the New River to provide 1,660 new homes for some of the worst housed of London's population. At Tulse Hill, Lambeth, on an area of 32 acres 500 modern flats had been erected and another 930 were under construction. In Bermondsey, 4,500 slum dwellers were having new dwellings built for them on a site of 21 acres, of which 5 acres would be devoted to open space. On the Mottingham Estate, 2,336 houses and flats had already been erected. Over a thousand houses and flats were built and occupied by the tenants on an estate in Lewisham which was intended to provide 74 acres of modern homes and well-planned shopping centres. Large-scale demolition and building operations were also going forward in Woolwich, Islington, Bethnal Green, St. Pancras, Clapham and other London boroughs.

To go on with details of sites, acres and buildings would mean turning several pages into something like an immense agent's catalogue. The position can be briefly stated. By 1938, in nearly every part of London where there were slums and overcrowding, those twin evils

Clearing Away the Slums

of the metropolis were being tackled to the utmost limit of the Council's resources. The face of London was changing. Dark hovels, crowded tenements, squalid rows of streets were being pulled down to make way for better and healthier dwellings.

The following table shows the extent of the slum clearance and rehousing programme carried out by the Labour Council between April 1934 and the outbreak of war in September 1939. A comparison is also provided between the performance of the Labour Council in five years and the performance of the Municipal Reform Council during their fifteen years of office from 1919 to 1934.

	Slum dwellers rehoused	Slum houses demolished
Labour in five years	82,999	12,652
Municipal Reform in fifteen years	17,144	4,460

In drawing this comparison it should be taken into account that it was not until about eighteen months after taking office that the Labour Council had begun to cut its way through the tangles of legal procedure and had succeeded in building up the staff and other resources required for the slum clearance campaign. Then when the drive was gathering momentum there came the increasing difficulties in the way of securing supplies of steel for building frameworks as the rearmament programme absorbed the limited supplies which were available. When these factors are taken into account it is clear beyond dispute that the Labour Council carried out a slum-clearance programme more extensive than any which London had ever seen before. Over 400 acres of slums—an area equal to the whole borough of Holborn—had been swept away to make room for new and well-planned homes.

During the course of the campaign against slums and overcrowding the Council built no less than 19,552 flats. But this was, however, only part of the total housing performance of the Council. In addition to the modern flat dwellings, the programme called for the building of new housing accommodation in the new industrial districts which were springing up around London. Complete housing estates were built at Mottingham, Whitefoot Lane, Hanwell, Kenmore and many other places on the perimeter of London.

During the same period of five years, in addition to the actual slum clearance programme, the Council provided 10,893 new houses on these estates.

In short, during a brief period of five years, the Labour Council provided over 30,000 new homes for Londoners with accommodation for over 125,000 people.

The standards set for this great housing programme were much higher than the minimum legal requirements. All the materials used in building construction, from bricks and mortar to nails and paint, had to pass the exacting scrutiny of the Council's technical experts and their inspectors on the sites.

The building plans incorporated many modern improvements in building technique and design. The Labour Party in opposition had consistently criticised the housing standards set for the Municipal Reformers' limited programmes—flats built with cramped interiors and a lack of modern amenities, as well as inferior standards of finish and decoration.

The Labour Council progressively improved the standard of design for flats and houses. A typical flat of the 1936 type, for example, had two bedrooms, a roomy living-room, kitchen, bathroom and separate lavatory. Metal windows opened wide to admit sunlight and air. In many flats the bathrooms were tiled and the baths were built in in the modern style. The kitchen had almost everything—good light and good cupboard room, a large hanging dresser, and was fitted with a gas water heater supplying hot water to sink and bathroom, and in many cases space was provided for a gas refrigerator which could be hired at a very low cost. A large number of the flats were provided with sun balconies large enough for the children or babies in prams to sleep out on during warm weather. The range of rents for these flats, exclusive of rates and water charges, was from about 5s. 6d. for a one-roomed flat with kitchen recess and bathroom, to 17s. 6d. for a five-roomed dwelling. There were private flats in London let at £250 and £300 a year which did not compare favourably with the flats built by the Council.

In all its plans for flats and houses the Council had regard to the fact that in providing homes it was in most cases also creating a community. Careful consideration was given in selecting sites to the proximity of schools, shopping centres, and other essential community services. On many of the sites, as for example at the great White City estate, the Council itself provided schools, playgrounds, churches, shops, inns and a community centre.

So much for the progress in the years before the war. The problems which faced the Labour majority in 1934, immense and complex though they were, shrink in comparison with the task of rebuilding and rehousing which confronts the London County Council today. The delapidations of time and the savage destruction of the enemy have created for London a housing problem of the utmost urgency.

Before the war, by far the greater part of London's inhabitants lived in houses which were unsuitable for modern life. Wartime neglect and structural damage by blast and concussion have hastened the process of decay and made them still more unsuitable for occupation from the viewpoint of health and convenience. Nearly a million houses are wearing the hasty patches of temporary war damage repairs and 70,000 houses have been completely wiped off the map of London. And once again, week by week, the pressure on London's dwelling-space is steadily increasing. The provision of homes for hundreds of thousands of Londoners is foremost among the many formidable problems which confront the Labour Council.

The Council was not unprepared for this peacetime emergency. While the debris from the blitz was still being cleared away, the Council asked their architect, Mr. J. H. Forshaw, and Professor Abercrombie to produce a plan for a better London, worthy of the people whose courage and endurance had won the admiration of the free world. The Council was determined that Londoners would get something more substantial than praise and promises. The architects were given a free hand to develop their conception of a London worthy of the people and equal to its place as the great capital city of the British Commonwealth.

Two years later the County of London Plan was published. There have been many plans produced by " planners " for the improvement of London. But, like Corbusier's plan for the reconstruction of Paris, these plans usually represented a triumph of geometry over the social and physical characteristics of London. There was a natural inclination when confronted with the appalling muddle and social complexities of London to " rub the whole place out, decant the population " and start all over again by drawing some neat geometric patterns on a clean sheet of paper.

There was nothing of this compass-and-ruler method about the plan produced by the Council's architect and

Clearing Away the Slums

Professor Abercrombie. The County of London Plan is not only an example of a great opportunity splendidly grasped, but it sets out a new concept for the planning, not only of London, but of all cities which will profoundly influence the work of planning all over the world.

The Plan set out to deal with the four great defects of London—depressed housing, traffic congestion, the lack of open spaces and the jumble of housing and industry. The Plan takes the chaotic tangle of endless streets, and shows how they can be made into modern communities based on those historic communities whose beginnings are to be found in the ancient villages of the London countryside. The Plan recognises the deep-rooted character of communities which like Whitechapel, Soho, and Limehouse have survived over centuries of London life. The Plan seeks to set these old associations in the new pattern of healthy and vigorous community life. This idea of community life is the great human factor which underlies the whole of the Plan.

These modern communities, with their civic centres, hospital and welfare services, and their segregated " industrial estates ", are broken up into " neighbourhood units " of 6,000 to 10,000 people with their own shopping centres, schools, social centres and other amenities.

The planners had to choose by what amount they should reduce the population in the overcrowded areas in order to provide reasonable living conditions in the new communities. If they had chosen to reduce density in these areas to 100 persons per acre, over half the people in many areas would have to be rehoused, mainly outside London. If they had chosen a density of 200 persons per acre, 20 per cent. of the people would have to be rehoused. The planners recommended the establishment of three principal density zones decreasing from the centre of 200, 136 and 100 persons an acre, which will require the reduction of the population by 39 per cent. At this density the Plan will enable 60 per cent. of the people to live in houses and 40 per cent. in flats over the whole area of the County.

In the new housing communities there will be a great variety in the layout and appearance of the houses so that the drab monotony of so much small-house development will be avoided. Some roads will be lined with paved or grassed forecourts to terraces behind which there will be access by paths to communal gardens where children can play in safety. In other parts of London there will be twentieth-century re-creations of the London squares with small gardens behind the houses, or groups of three-and-four-story flats, and communal gardens in the middle of the squares. Around the dwellings, whether in flats or houses, there will be large parks with ample space for allotments and recreations.

The Plan proposes to remedy the choked chaos of London's traffic by great radial and arterial roads around and through London which would draw off the fast long-distance traffic, and preserve the local communities from the interference of through traffic.

Certain areas of London, the Government, University and Museum quarters, would become great " precincts " sealed to all traffic except that which has business within.

The plan proposes to unravel the confusion of industry and housing in many parts of London. Industry must be more evenly distributed over the County so that no part remains an unhealthy huddle of houses and factories, and the industry in any community must be grouped in " Trading Estates ". The Plan suggests that the factories in these estates might possibly be built by a new form of " public utility " or even by the local authorities themselves. There will be restaurants and rest rooms in

Clearing Away the Slums

the factories and adequate open spaces and gardens between them.

The Plan recognises, however, that no citizen's life should be confined to the area of his " community ". This new metropolis, with its various communities, its open spaces and parklands, its underground railway system, its precincts, terraces and segregated " Trading Estates ", is planned to form one organic whole—the great commonalty of London. The great imperial city is woven together, by the passage of men and women in their business and their pleasure, possessing a livelier consciousness of the unity of London and with a civic pride which is fostered by the awareness of community and fellowship in their own smaller areas.

Sufficient has been said to show the vision and scope of the Plan for a better and healthier London. Its great merit is to be found not only in the technical brilliance of many of the proposals but in its unique emphasis on the fact that the Plan must be made to fit the people, instead of the people being called upon to adjust themselves to the arbitrary requirements of the planner's judgement. The planners themselves emphasise this theme as the dominant characteristic of their work. They state that " social facts are primary, and the physical organisation of a city, its industries and markets, its lines of communication and traffic, must be subservient to social needs ".

This idea, that the needs and interests of the people are the first consideration in all aspects of the work of a local authority, was the theme which constantly reoccurs in all the work which Labour did for London.

The County of London Plan was submitted by the Council for consideration to those whom it most concerned, the people of London. Full details were made available in a book, and by brochures and public exhibitions. At the same time the Council entered into discussions with the Metropolitan Borough Councils and other interested bodies. It was in the light of all these discussions that the Plan came before the whole Council on Tuesday, 17th July 1945. In spite of all the immense difficulties which lay in the path of its attainment, the Labour Council boldly accepted the Plan as the method of building a new and far better city for all the people of London.

The following is an extract from the recommendations of the Town Planning Committee presented by Mr. Lewis Silkin, as they were accepted by the Council.

The County of London Plan must be carried out in a series of stages self-contained as far as practicable yet interrelated to form a scheme of progressive realisation of the whole. We are preparing a programme for the first 10 years covering various aspects of the Plan, together with a list of works for a shorter period.

We have endeavoured . . . to give some indication of the greatness, the complexity and the manifold difficulties of the planning task which faces the Council in the coming years and of the principles upon which, in our view, it should be undertaken.

Many difficulties remain to be resolved ; many issues require further clarification and consideration before they can be finally settled. Nevertheless, we are convinced that the essential principles we set out form a sound basis from which to launch a sustained assault upon the immense task which confronts the Council as a leading municipal authority responsible for influencing and controlling the physical development of one of the world's greatest metropolitan areas—an area which has not only suffered unusually heavy damage, but which provides an embodiment of the endeavour, the hope and the affection of the whole British people.

It is our conviction that any difficulties which may beset the fulfilment of that duty must lead not to resigned inactivity, but to an effort commensurate with the present unexampled opportunity, to regenerate the great structure of London, to

Clearing Away the Slums

emphasise in it what is worthy of the great past, and to eradicate that which is unworthy.

Once before in the history of London an opportunity presented itself to build a great city worthy of its place, its traditions and its citizens. After the Great Fire of London the far-reaching vision of Wren and Evelyn grasped at the opportunity of creating a city of wide streets, splendid squares and noble buildings. Their plans never reached the threshold of fulfilment, and many generations have paid a heavy price for the narrow streets and mean and crowded buildings which private greed and narrow vested interests built in place of the commodious and splendid city which Wren had designed. A hundred years ago the Commissioners for Improving the metropolis remarked regretfully that the fate of Wren's plans demonstrates " the difficulty of effecting great and systematic changes in such a metropolis. They were thwarted by public bodies and individual interests."

Wren's conception of a new London was buried beneath a huddle of mean streets. We stand again on the threshold of an immense opportunity for the reconstruction of London. The forces of self-interest are still powerful to thwart, delay and obstruct this new project for the betterment of London. The achievement of this better planned, healthier and more splendid London will largely depend on the co-operation, and on the vigilance, of all its citizens.

Chapter VI

A GREAT EXPERIMENT IN SOCIAL WELFARE

IF the London Labour Party were to be judged by its record in the fields of Public Assistance alone it would still be able to claim the credit for an outstanding social achievement.

Within a few weeks of coming to power the Labour Council had put an end to the long and bitter conflict which had centred around the question of poor relief in the metropolis. The harsh and repressive attitude which regarded poverty as a crime was replaced by a more enlightened outlook. But this change did not stop short at a more generous interpretation of human needs. Within a few years a great forward move had taken place over the whole field of Poor Law administration in London. The bleak and grudging system of Public Assistance gave place to the more constructive outlook which regarded the provision of relief as a Social Welfare Service.

In order to assess what was achieved in this field we must take a swift backward glance at the administration of relief in the metropolis. London, like the rest of England, got its first system of poor relief from the Act of Elizabeth in 1601 which laid the responsibility of providing for the poor on the parish in which they lived. But the burden of poverty in London has always been unequally distributed. Some parishes had to provide for a large number of the " lame, impotent, old, blind, and such other among them being poor and not able to work ", while the wealthier parishes levied only a very small poor rate, or even none at all, on their inhabitants.

The Poor Law Act of 1834 set up elected Boards of

A Great Experiment in Social Welfare

Guardians to establish " Union Workhouses " by means of a compulsory union of parishes for that purpose. But in London even these larger units of administration were still too small to carry the burdens which were thrust upon them. The new Act laid down that the able-bodied poor were no longer entitled to outdoor relief but had to come into the union workhouses. The rapid growth of London at this period was continually pushing up the amount of destitution in the poorer districts, and, as more and more people were forced into the workhouses, the already depressed standards of diet and accommodation were forced down to grossly inhuman levels.

Then, in 1865, the spectre of disease became, yet once again, the successful advocate of reform. In 1853-4 over eleven thousand people in the metropolis had died of cholera. In 1864 there were increasing signs that another epidemic was on the way. *The Times* began to campaign that the workhouses were the centres of infection and published almost daily reports of the inquests on the paupers who had died of inhumanity and neglect in the workhouses. A commission of three medical men appointed by the *Lancet* published a report which exposed the appalling living and sanitary conditions of the paupers inside the workhouses. The inhuman treatment of the sick and the destitute was shown to possess the elements of a dreadful retribution.

Fear proved a more powerful advocate than the claims of humanity or the promptings of conscience. So far as London was concerned, the system was altered immediately by the Metropolitan Poor Act of 1867, which created a Common Poor Fund, and on the basis of fivepence a day for each inmate of the workhouse, a general poor rate was levied over the whole of the Metropolitan area. Furthermore, financed out of the same general rate, a new authority, the Metropolitan Asylums Board, was created to maintain hospitals and asylums. It should be noted, however, that persons receiving outdoor relief could not be charged to the Common Poor Fund, and a formidable financial barrier was thus erected against a Board of Guardians following more humane policies in the administration of poor relief.

For over a half-century this system of Poor Law administration remained unaltered in any of its main aspects. The principle of " no relief for the able-bodied outside the workhouse " was rigidly enforced. The poor were hustled into the workhouses. Families were ruthlessly broken up, husbands and wives were separated, children were taken away from their parents. Conditions inside the workhouses were deliberately made as bleak and degrading as possible. The great mass of working men and their wives and children came to consider the road to the Union Workhouses as more dreadful than the one which lead to the gates of the cemetery itself.

The spasmodic revolts of the poor against the iron rule of the Poor Law, the pleadings of the benevolent, and the urging of Royal Commissioners secured no relaxation of the system. The famous Royal Commission on the Poor Law which reported in 1909 gave special attention to the problems of London. The Commission pointed out that the London Unions, as separate and distinct organisations, had not been able to adapt themselves to the needs of the metropolis. The variations in rateable value, as compared with the needs of the population, had made it very difficult to establish a common standard of treatment. Their enquiries into the policy, practice, scale of relief, and costs of institutions had shown a wide divergence between the different Unions and sometimes between Unions immediately adjacent to each other. The Royal Commission unanimously urged that the first

A Great Experiment in Social Welfare 115

essential reform was the total abolition of the Boards of Guardians and the establishment of a unified London for all purposes of Poor Law administration.

The Minority Report of the Commission, with which the name of Beatrice Webb is associated, while concurring in the need for a unified system of relief for London, went on to urge the even more comprehensive reform of the complete break up of the existing Poor Law, and the transfer of many of its functions to committees of the County and County Borough authorities.

Nothing was done about any of these recommendations, but after the First World War, the then existing Ministry of Reconstruction appointed the Maclean Commission to conduct another enquiry into the machinery of the Poor Law. This Commission, like its predecessor, again urged the abolition of the Boards of Guardians, pointing out that they were faced by " overlapping functions and areas and by conflicting principles of administration ".

By 1921 the post-war boom had exhausted itself and the country was sliding down into the first of the cycles of depression which became the main feature of our economy in the years between the wars. There was a rush of unemployed people to the relieving officers. The number in receipt of Poor Relief in London increased eightfold from 23,352 in 1920 to 185,889 in 1922. Under the existing system of administration the Boards of Guardians had the alternative of cramming the unemployed into the workhouses, and so spreading the charge over the whole metropolitan area, or of giving outdoor relief at the expense of raising the local poor rate to intolerable levels. Poplar faced this intractable problem by deciding to grant a large measure of outdoor relief, and when the local poor rate had soared to an alarming figure the Poplar Council refused to levy the London County Council precept on the grounds that their rates, without it, were already more than the people could bear. The Poplar councillors went to jail for their failure to comply with the law, but on the other hand the Government were forced to pass an Act which made outdoor relief a charge on the Common Poor Fund.

It is not possible to give any detailed account of the struggles which centred around the question of Public Assistance in London. The political controversies, the long struggle that was waged between the Ministry of Health and the Labour Boards of Guardians, the successive Government "cuts" in unemployment benefits and relief, the misery and suffering of increasing numbers of the British people are outside the limits of the present account. By 1928 the pressure on the machinery of Public Assistance had become acute. The rising wave of unemployment was forcing an intolerable burden on the existing system of administration. Twenty years after the first Royal Commission had published its report the Government accepted its recommendation to supersede the Boards of Guardians. The Local Government Act of 1929, which contained this element of reform, was made palatable to the Conservative interests by provisions which allowed the complete derating of agricultural land and the partial derating of industrial premises.

In one respect the reform thus effected was a further development of that carried out by the Act of 1834. As the parish had then become too small a unit, so now had the Union, and it was superseded by the County and County Borough authorities, and the duties and assets of the Boards of Guardians were transferred to them.

The Labour Party had supported the recommendation of Minority Report of the 1909 Poor Law Commission calling for the complete break-up of the Poor Law System, and the London Labour Party since its inception had strongly urged the need for centralising the administra-

A Great Experiment in Social Welfare

tion of Poor Relief in London. The 1929 Act was, therefore, welcomed by the Labour Party as providing the opportunity for carrying out great and necessary reforms in the administration of poor relief in London. The break-up of the Poor Law had at last become a possibility. Under the Act the Council had wide powers to decide which of the Poor Law services could be transferred to other committees of the Council. For example, the Poor Law schools and training establishments could be brought under the control of the Education Committee. The vast " general mixed workhouses " which, under the existing system, catered for the able-bodied unemployed and their dependants, the active old folk, the semi-helpless aged people, and even the children of inmates, could now have their inmates classified and distributed to the hospitals, special homes, schools, training centres and other branches of the Council's services where they could receive the effective treatment, care or assistance they might require. In addition to this allocation to other services, two other very important reforms were also made possible. In place of the wide difference in Poor Law administration in London, it was now possible to establish for the metropolis a general standard in the measure of assistance, without, however, running to the other extreme of a crude uniformity in " scales " of relief which took no account of individual needs. Secondly, the transfer to the Council of the infirmaries attached to the workhouses and the hospitals and asylums under the Metropolitan Asylums Board made it possible to provide London with the largest and most comprehensive Municipal Hospital Service of any city in the world.

The magnitude of the task which was assumed by the Council can be judged by the statement of the Chairman of the Council on 1st April, 1930 :

Labour in London

From midnight last night we took over and became responsible for the administration of some thirty different authorities—140 hospitals, schools and other institutions, 75,000 beds and about 180,000 people who are in receipt of relief. The services of some 26,000 additional staff will be utilised in various capacities, and these figures alone indicate the magnitude of the extension of our duties and liabilities demanding co-ordinative management.

It is an immense tribute to the efficiency and capacity of the London County Council staff that this vast and complicated transfer was swiftly and smoothly carried out.

It must be frankly admitted that the prospect of the wide reforms which had become possible seemed to have touched the imaginations of the Municipal Reform majority on the Council. The scheme submitted by them to the Ministry of Health provided for the immediate transfer of many of the existing Poor Law functions to other services of the Council. Any criticism of the scheme was concerned with points of detail; as a whole, it undoubtedly represented a most comprehensive and thoroughgoing reform of the existing system of poor relief administration in the metropolis. In so far as the actual administration of relief was concerned, the Municipal Reform Party declared that no attempt would be made to enforce a standard " scale " of relief for the whole of London, but that the individual needs of applicants would be fully taken into account in assessing the amount of relief.

We have no reason for doubting the honesty and good intentions of the Municipal Reformers when they first propounded their schemes and proposals for dealing with poor relief in London. The Council announced its intention of pressing ahead with various improvements in the many institutions under its care; the work of

A Great Experiment in Social Welfare 119

co-ordinating the hospitals and their allied services into a comprehensive municipal health service was pressed ahead. For a while it certainly did appear that the Municipal Reformers had at last caught up with more enlightened and progressive standards of civic behaviour.

Unfortunately, it turned out that this period was, after all, no more than the brief " St. Martin's Summer " of reform. All these, and a great many other improvements, were suddenly swallowed up by the panic pleas for economy issued by the newly formed " National " Government in 1931. Enlightened policies vanished overnight. The Municipal Reformers wielded the axe of economy swiftly and ruthlessly over all the principal services of the Council. Three-quarters of a million pounds were scraped off the current estimates, the capital expenditure was cut by half, and the rates were brought down by 11d. in the £. This financial result was claimed as a civic triumph, without any reckoning of the havoc which had been wrought in the social services and the heartbreak and bitterness in thousands of lives by the policy of reckless and unthinking economy. And nowhere were the economies more bitterly and intensely felt than among the thousands of unemployed who were being compelled in increasing numbers to apply to the relieving officers of the Council.

In opposing these headlong cuts and economies, the Labour Party on the Council pointed out, again and again, that apart even from the human considerations involved, the policy of drastic economy was defeating its own aims by still further restricting purchasing power and thereby accentuating the general trade depression. The London Labour Party advocated the policy of carrying out a series of important and necessary improvements, such as the reconstruction of Wandsworth Bridge and the road-widening schemes which would eliminate the wasteful bottlenecks in London traffic. These proposals were denounced as "financial lunacy" which would promote national disaster. This was, of course, thirteen years before a Government White Paper on Full Employment envisaged such schemes of expenditure by local authorities as an essential element in "maintaining a high and stable level of employment." The Ray Report, the May Report, Ramsay MacDonald, the whole Tory Party, the experts at the Treasury and the professional economists all thought otherwise.

The declared policy of the Municipal Reformers of ensuring that the amount of relief should be adjusted to the needs of the applicants was abandoned in practice. This principle was never openly repudiated, but the Municipal Reform members who comprised the majority of the Public Assistance Committees received instructions to operate a uniform "scale" of relief which precluded any real consideration being given to the true need of applicants. The Municipal Reformers did not possess sufficient courage to withdraw their promises, but they were unable to rebut the continued accusations of the Labour Councillors that

word had been passed to the members of the majority Party on the various district sub-committees to cut down relief to the very bone, and in numerous cases where families were living almost on the verge of starvation on relief granted by the Public Assistance Committee such relief has been still further reduced.[1]

For the next three years the poor were harried like criminals. All the subtle ingenuity of skilled legal minds was brought to bear on ascertaining ways and means of securing new economies at the expense of the least fortunate of London's citizens. Attempts were made to

[1] *London Labour Party Report*, 1931–2.

A Great Experiment in Social Welfare 121

force the responsibilities on to other members* of the family. For example, when a grown-up son applied for relief he was told that because his father and mother were receiving public assistance, he must live on the amount given to his father and mother, although his needs had not been taken into account when the Sub-Committee had assessed his parents' allowance. The full incomes of all members of the household were taken into account in assessing the amount of relief, irrespective of the amount which they were actually able to contribute to the household. Many families were broken up by that ruling. In the face of a rising storm of protests, the majority rejected Labour's demand for the reasonable provision of fuel for people on relief during the bitter winter seasons. Contrary to the provisions of Section 48 of the Poor Law, which provided that Friendly Society Sick Pay up to 5s. and Health Insurance up to 7s. 6d. should not be taken into account in granting outdoor relief, the Municipal Reform Party issued instructions that these amounts should none the less be taken into account in deciding whether any relief to sick people was necessary at all. Married men were compelled to leave their families and go to training camps like the one at Hollesley Bay.

For three years these harsh and drastic policies of Public Assistance administration were enforced in the metropolis. An appalling picture of the conditions of existence to which many applicants of relief were reduced emerges from the last debate which the Labour Party forced on the Council in November 1933, a few months before the election which swept the Tory majority and their policies from power.

Mr. Hayward, who, as the first Labour Chairman of the Public Assistance Committee, was to have the task of reversing many of the Municipal Reform policies, introduced a motion which condemned the policy of the Public Assistance Committees in (1) reducing the relief granted to old people, (2) enforcing a continuous reduction in the amounts of outdoor relief, (3) refusing to deal reasonably with the claims for the supplementation of unemployment relief, (4) unjustly administering the means test, (5) indiscriminately ordering married men on outdoor relief to residential training centres, and (6) taking into account unfairly and improperly the earnings of other members of the household.

The case which this Labour councillor presented to the Council was full, precise and substantiated with detailed instances. It provided a startling glimpse of the levels of starvation and humiliation to which thousands of people were being systematically reduced in the wealthiest city in the world.

Mr. Hayward described how old people were being deprived of the supplementary allowance of up to 6s. which they were entitled to receive in addition to the old age pension of 10s. The consequence was that many of these old people were compelled to give up their rooms, go into institutions, or become dependent on their relatives for support.

He quoted from the instructions of the Council to the relieving officers to show the incredibly mean and degrading strategems which were practised on those in receipt of relief. For example, officers were instructed to

call at meal times to see that applicants are having separate food. In other words, if the woman upstairs happens to be down-stairs talking to her friend on the next floor, and is invited to have a cup of tea when the officer calls, she would lose her relief. It is said that where a separate coal allowance is given, the relieving officer should be satisfied that a separate fire is provided. If two old people are living together and getting a small amount of relief, they must have a separate fire or there will be only one coal allowance.

A Great Experiment in Social Welfare 123

Mr. Lewis Silkin, speaking later in the debate—and not even his bitterest opponents will accuse him of any tendency towards exaggeration—summarised the general position when he stated that

> applicants for relief were treated like dirt, and as people who probably had secret resources but were pretending to be destitute. Public Assistance Committees considered that they had done something praiseworthy if applicants could be fobbed off with something less than they were entitled to, and people were being deterred from applying. One of the worst deterrent practices was to tell people they would get nothing unless they went into a residential institution for an indefinite period. Cases had come to his notice where families had been broken up through the husband being sent to a residential institution.

Sir Cyril Cobb, the Tory Chairman of the Public Assistance Committee, took less than three minutes to reply to the fully substantiated and serious allegations of the Labour Councillors. Amid shouts of protest, he declared that it was " not necessary to go into the points raised today. They will all be brought up again nearer the time when the electorate will have to settle this question between us and the people opposite."

As we know, the electorate did settle this question—and many others—very decisively at the elections in March 1934. The responsibility for the administration of Public Assistance in London was taken out of the repressive hands of the Municipal Reformers and transferred to the Labour majority on the Council.

The changes which were made by the Labour majority were immediate and far-reaching. It would be idle, however, to pretend that the Labour councillors waved some compelling wand over the whole system of Public Assistance and transformed its methods and outlook overnight. Neither Herbert Morrison nor Mr. Hayward, the Chairman of the Public Assistance Committee, and the other labour members of the Council possessed that sort of social alchemy. In a previous chapter we have indicated some of the limits within which a local authority can move, and in the realm of Public Assistance these limits are sharply marked by enactment and circumstances. In the first place, the social surgery necessary to reach the root causes of poverty in our society was not within the scope of a local authority. Then, too, a system which had been adapted to treating the poor, in Lewis Silkin's phrase, " like dirt," could not be transformed suddenly into the instrument of a better social purpose. A repressive tradition dies slowly.

But even when these qualifications have been stated, the changes which the Labour Party were able to introduce were considerable and far-reaching in their influence. The harsh measures and stringent economies had, at a cost of incredible suffering and misery, resulted in a saving of a few thousand pounds. But the pence and shillings which had been pared off the allowances of those dependent on relief had a measure of value which it is not easy for the more affluent to estimate. A penny could keep the gas-stove alight while the dinner was cooked. Threepence could provide a pint of milk for hungry babies. A shilling in a cheap market could buy, in 1933, enough meat to make a reasonable dinner for four people. A penny, threepence and a shilling became very high denominators of value when viewed from that angle. In taking immediate steps, therefore, to ensure that in all cases relief was more closely adjusted to individual needs, the Labour Council was raising an immense burden of misery and anxiety from thousands of lives.

The report of the Public Assistance Committee to the Council in June 1934 illustrates the change in spirit and method which had overtaken the administration of poor

A Great Experiment in Social Welfare 125

relief in the metropolis within the short space of three months.

The increase in the numbers on relief during the June quarter 1934 (approximately 11,000), reflects, we feel, the fact that in recent years, under the previous administration, many persons were refused relief who, in our opinion, should not have been excluded, and this statement covers the cases of unemployed men who were refused relief in supplementation of unemployment insurance benefit or transitional payment, although by the normal standards of the district sub-committees in question the family income was insufficient for the family needs. Further, many persons on relief were not, in our opinion, receiving sufficient for their reasonable human requirements.

The higher amounts of relief now being granted include an increased allowance for dependent children and a fuller recognition of the immediate difficulties of families who are suffering from the burden of high or excessive rents. Both the increase in numbers on relief and the increase in the average amount given are due to a further change in policy to which the attention of the Council should be called, namely, the reasonable treatment of the earning children whose earnings are taken into account in calculating the household income. The practise of making careful investigation into the amount of household income, as required by the Relief Regulations Order, 1930, has been maintained, and allowance has continued to be made for a contribution by earning members, but we consider it desirable that earning children should be allowed a reasonable margin for personal expense, clothing and recreation.

The first urgent necessity of making the relief given to applicants " sufficient for their reasonable human requirements " was thus achieved by the first act of the Labour Council. Other improvements followed swiftly on. The regulations of the Tory Council requiring relieving officers to take into account a proportion of the Friendly Society Sick Pay and Health Benefit were rescinded on the grounds that sick people would need the margin of a few shillings for extra nourishment and other requirements. The allowances for all old age pensioners were increased, a coal allowance was provided for them throughout the year, and these aged people were no longer forced into institutions or driven to depend on their relatives by the withholding of their supplementary rent allowances. Within the limits of the Poor Law Act, the standards of relief afforded to applicants were, during the ten years of Labour's administration, adjusted to a more equitable basis on a number of occasions to meet changing circumstances.

It would be a mistake, however, to assume that the new attitude towards relief was based on the giving of *largesse* out of the public funds with little sense of responsibility. A policy of relief based on the indiscriminate doling out of public funds would defeat its own aims. It was obviously not in the interests of the community that the relief granted should be such that the recipient was discouraged from striving to gain his independence, or that it should induce others to fall back on the same system of relief. On the other hand, the Labour Party has stated no less emphatically that it was also not in the interests of the community that the relief given should be so grossly inadequate that the repressed standards of living unfitted men for employment, imposed intolerable household burdens on their womenfolk and resulted in the serious malnutrition of their children.

The statistics show that the new human policies of relief were not based on any financial extravagance or the reckless expenditure of public money. The average weekly number of persons in receipt of outdoor relief during Labour's first year of office was 105,124—an increase of 8,088 over the average for the last year of Tory administration. During 1934–5 the total amount of relief granted by the Labour Council was £1,961,103.

A Great Experiment in Social Welfare

This total compares with £1,605,272 for 1933-4 and £1,630,673 for 1932-3. The increase in expenditure represented less than one per cent. of the total L.C.C. expenditure for 1934-5.

But the reform of the system of Public Assistance in London went a long way further than the provision of more adequate standards of relief. An effective policy of relief administration must be broader and deeper than its financial provisions. The next step towards an improved system of administration in London was to rid the service of the atmosphere, outlook and methods of the nineteenth-century Poor Law with its "deterrent" practices and penal provisions. New regulations were drafted which, while preserving necessary safeguards, abolished the deliberately penal aspects of relief. For example, in other than exceptional cases, married men were no longer separated from their families and sent for long periods to residential training centres. In fact, within a few months of Labour coming into power, 300 married men in the training centres were returned to their homes.

The maintenance of these training centres was enjoined by Article 6 of the Poor Relief Regulation Order, 1930, which required the Council to make arrangements for all able-bodied men in receipt of relief to be "set to work, trained or instructed". It was consistent with the new policy that the Labour Council should emphasise in its arrangements the educative aspect of the statute.

In developing its arrangements under Article 6 of the Order the Council has provided for the training and instruction of the men rather than for setting them to work. The main object of the training centres is to maintain the employability of men and assist in their restoration to independent life and there is a complete absence of the deterrent or semi-penal methods of bygone days, which were denoted by the term "test work", a term which is quite out of place in reference to the present arrangements.[1]

The methods of instruction in the centres were brought into line with this statement of policy. The hours of attendance at the non-residential centres were reduced from 30 to 20, so that the mornings were kept free for the search for work. Where practicable the men were allowed to choose the classes which they wished to attend. Most of the classes were directed at enabling them to improve their existing skill, or else equip them with an entirely new trade or occupation for earning their living —motor repair work, upholstery, chairmaking, land work, and hairdressing were among the many subjects provided in the classes. General educational subjects and physical training helped to tone up relaxed bodies and minds. No man was required, however, to receive training or instruction if he objected to doing so ; instead, he was given useful work to do in and about the centre.

These changes marked a profound alteration of method and outlook so far as the training centres were concerned. In other aspects of relief other improvements were carried out in order to remove the last vestiges of the penal Poor Law tradition. It had, for example, been the degrading practice to give applicants for outdoor relief " food tickets " which they had to exchange for their requirements with the local tradesman. People who were forced to apply for assistance after long years of self-respecting independence were usually very conscious of their position, and their mental suffering was considerably increased by the public disclosure to their neighbours and shopkeepers of what they regarded as a very humili-

---

[1] L.C.C. Public Assistance Committee, *The Administration of Relief* (P.A.6), p. 39.

A Great Experiment in Social Welfare 129

ating position. Under the Tory administration of 1932-3 nearly a quarter of the total outdoor relief was given as " relief in kind ". The Labour Council immediately cut down the amount of relief in kind from these degrading proportions. It was laid down as the general policy of the Public Assistance Committee that relief should be granted in cash in all cases in which the applicants were persons of good character. The Committee, in deciding on this policy, comments that " there is no reason why such persons should not be trusted to make the best use of cash relief, and it is frequently urged that they can, in fact, make better use of the money in their purchase of food than they can of food tickets ". Within a year the amount of relief in kind was slashed from a quarter of the total to less than five per cent., and in his annual report to the Council the Chief Officer of Public Assistance remarked that there was " no reason to believe that the diminution of relief in kind has been abused ".

Other changes followed which were in keeping with the new spirit of public assistance administration. Many of the local offices and relief stations under the management of the Public Assistance Committee were bare, cold and forbidding. Applicants had to wait long hours in draughty corridors and bleak rooms. These offices were completely redecorated and modernised ; in several areas completely new offices were erected, and steps were taken to reduce to a minimum the waiting period before applicants were interviewed by officers and committees.

We cannot follow in detail the other reforms and improvements which the Labour Council introduced into the administration of outdoor relief. Enough has been told to show the spirit which directed the work of reform. The main Public Assistance Committee initiated and guided these developments, but the hundreds of Labour men and women who served on the 29 local sub-committees and the 99 district sub-committees were themselves responsible for the speed and thoroughness with which the old methods and outlook of the Poor Law were swept away. Before March 1934, these committees had been manned by a majority which shared the outlook of the Municipal Reformers on Public Assistance, and had been responsible for operating the "shadow scales" of relief. These committees were reconstituted in March 1934, and applicants for relief before the local committees now found themselves facing men and women who were not inspired by a harsh parsimony and who were not prepared to treat applicants for relief as social malingerers with secret financial resources. For many of those who had previous experience of the committees, the change was almost too startling to be believed.

The changes introduced in the system of institutional relief were no less comprehensive. Many of the workhouses taken over from the Boards of Guardians were veritable "Bastilles of poverty". They were grim, forbidding buildings, bleak and chill, and often lacking in any modern comforts and conveniences. Waterloo House in Bethnal Green, for example, had been originally designed as a barracks during the Napoleonic wars. The Labour Council promptly decided that this building was no longer suitable for housing the aged and infirm and Waterloo House was closed and the site used for a housing scheme.

Most people regard the workhouse as providing for the able-bodied destitute and aged people who were no longer able to work. But these were only two of the many classes of inmate which were to be found in the London workhouses in 1934. These bleak barracks absorbed many sorts and conditions of men. The misfits and failures of our society, the lame, the aged, the

A Great Experiment in Social Welfare

chronic sick, the undersized and the deformed, the able-bodied unemployed, the deserted wife and her babies, the family which suddenly found itself in the street owing to fire, flood or eviction, the unmarried mother who had no home, people who, without being certifiable, had mental weaknesses or faults of character which prevented them earning their livings—this was the indiscriminate assortment of human beings who found themselves sharing the same roof and under the same system of administration.

The mixed general workhouse fitted the social outlook which assessed the value of a human being on the basis of the capacity to work and produce. Within its walls there might be no active cruelty or deliberate neglect. But the conditions were utterly static. Under a uniform system of administration there could be little active interest in the diverse needs of all the different categories of inmate. After a lifetime of maintaining their own home, aged people found themselves under the same roof as the half-imbecile adult and the less reputable discards of society. In these circumstances there was little incentive or opportunity for providing the aged with those additional comforts and amenities which matter so much to the old people, nor, on the other hand, could there be adequate provision for the care of the sick, or the training and treatment of those who might again be fitted to take their part as self-respecting members of the community.

The Labour Party on the Council had insisted that the mixed workhouse should be abolished, and that the classes of inmate should be grouped according to their needs and provided with accommodation suitable to their requirements. Within a few months of coming into power the Labour Council had adopted proposals which marked the end of the mixed workhouse in London.

Labour in London

The first and most important step was to pass on to the other services of the Council those persons and institutions most suitable for their care. People in need of constant medical attention were transferred to the hospitals, mental cases were brought under the care of special homes or the appropriate mental hospital, and all " Poor Law " maternity cases were transferred to the more fitting care of the hospitals and Medical Services Committee.

After this initial sorting out of inmates, the Public Assistance Committee was able to begin the second stage of remodelling the system of institutional relief. It was decided that able-bodied men should be housed in separate institutions which should be training centres instead of being, as it were, static workhouses. Mothers and babies were to be accommodated in nursery homes. Finally, it was decided that old people who were likely to spend the rest of their lives in the Council's care should have a quiet retreat removed from the bustling and unsettling atmosphere of the big institution, and the scheme of re-organisation therefore provided for the removal of all these old people to small homes where close attention could be given to their comfort and convenience.

The details of the carrying out of this scheme of re-organisation are beyond the scope of this book. The programme called for the construction of a number of new homes, nurseries and hostels and the modernising of the bleak and dilapidated institutions. All of these institutions were completely re-equipped. Long tables and benches were replaced by small tables and chairs, living-rooms and bedrooms were made more colourful and homelike by substituting light colour schemes for the drab browns of the old workhouse walls. Pictures appeared on the walls, casement curtains on the windows,

A Great Experiment in Social Welfare 133

and chintz counterpanes in gay colours were provided for the bedrooms. The radio came to banish the dull apathy of the old workhouse dayroom, recreations were provided. The colour, comfort and conveniences of the modern age invaded the bleak and colourless monotony of the Poor Law " Bastilles " with incalculable effects on the minds of the staff and inmates.

Where practicable, the high workhouse walls, which had the appearance of shutting the institution off from the community, were pulled down. The purely repressive regulations were abolished. The old and infirm were given liberal opportunity of going out to meet their friends. The clothes of inmates were no longer made of a distinct cloth and cut which marked them off from the rest of the community. The standards of diet were considerably improved.

Even the " dosser " was not forgotten. The hand of humanity and fellowship reached down into the harsh and bleak atmosphere of the London Casual Wards. Improved methods of administration were adopted, the food was amplified, the facilities extended. The statement that " the casual vagrant is beyond redemption " was proved another convenient figment of a social creed which is always eager to blame " human nature " instead of the defects of the existing system of society.

Significant of the changed outlook and methods in the administration of public relief was the decision taken by the Council in 1940, to discard the use of the title " Public Assistance." Henceforth, this duty of the Council towards the great capital's less fortunate citizens would be discharged through its Social Welfare Committee. In word, as well as in deed, a grim era in social administration in London had been finally brought to a close.

CHAPTER VII

A MUNICIPAL HEALTH SERVICE

FIFTY years ago the family doctor could carry all the medical equipment he needed in his little black bag. The stethoscope and the clinical thermometer were the principal instruments of medical diagnosis. The apparatus of the surgeon was hardly any more complicated. In the previous hundred years the use of antiseptics and anaesthetics were the two outstanding discoveries, and both of them had simplified rather than complicated the work of medical and surgical treatment.

Within twenty years the situation had been radically changed. The physicist, the biochemist, the electrician and the medical specialist had swiftly opened up new methods of diagnosis and treatment. Many of these new methods called for the use of complicated equipment which occupied a lot of room and cost a large amount of money. A complete X-ray unit might cost as much as £50,000 and required many thousand pounds a year to maintain. An ounce of radium cost more than a ton of gold, and its fierce potency had to be controlled by expensive equipment and highly skilled technicians. Electro-cardiograms which recorded the hidden pulses of the heart cost several thousand pounds apiece. The solarium, with its healing rays of actinic light, demanded expensive equipment and considerable sums for its upkeep. A great deal of money had to be spent in equipping the laboratories of the pathologist and the bio-chemist. Hormones, vaccines, and sera demonstrated their compelling mastery over many intractable complaints and diseases, but they cost a lot of money.

More potent drugs and safer anaesthetics increased the

A Municipal Health Service

physicians control over the forces of disease and decay. Many more powerful and more delicate instruments supplied new eyes and fingers to the surgeon. But each advance had its money price. And the money which was poured so abundantly into the speculations of the Stock Exchange slowed to a thin trickle when it came to the matter of the struggle against death and disease.

As the cost of medical treatment increased, the Voluntary Hospitals in London, dependent upon the endowments and subscriptions of the charitable-minded, found themselves waging an interminable struggle to provide the necessary standards of treatment and to make ends meet. All kinds of devices were adopted to raise the necessary funds—flag days, street collectors, draws, lotteries, film shows and workmen's contributions. Still the funds lagged a long way behind requirements. Some of the hospitals had to turn their public wards, originally intended under the Royal Charters for the " sick poor ", into paying wards to secure the money needed to keep the hospital going. In 1929, 49 per cent. of the income of King's College Hospital, for example, was derived from paying patients. In the same year, there were approximately 10,000 people waiting for admission to the London hospitals. Many of them had been waiting for months and some of them even for years.

In an article in the *Lancet* of the 3rd August 1939, a famous surgeon gave his experienced estimate of the position of the voluntary hospitals in London.

Far from our hospitals being, as they once were, the envy of other nations, the great majority are years behind the times and lack of funds compels the hospitals of our Metropolis to carry on their work in the heart of London with an equipment and in surroundings which would not be tolerated in a small provincial town in Sweden.

So much for the Voluntary Hospitals where medical

progress was dependent on private benevolence and on the increasing use of the system of " paying beds ". A Londoner unable to become a paying patient or to secure priority on the waiting lists of the Voluntary Hospitals was compelled to have recourse to the " Poor Law " infirmaries of the Board of Guardians. A few of these infirmaries were fairly adequately equipped, but the great majority of them fell far below modern requirements. Over them all hung the atmosphere of the Poor Law tradition. Apart from the taint of the Poor Law, these infirmaries had the grave defect that no provision was made for out-patient treatment, and a patient on discharge from the infirmary had often to find his way into the already overcrowded out-patients' departments of the Voluntary Hospitals.

In addition to these infirmaries of the Boards of Guardians, there were the special hospitals for infectious diseases maintained by the Metropolitan Asylums Board, and the few special and mental hospitals of the London County Council.

Against this background we can visualise how great was the opportunity created by the Local Government Act of 1929 which transferred to the London County Council all the hospitals and medical services carried on by the twenty-five Boards of Guardians and the Metropolitan Asylums Board. The Council had already been responsible for certain preventive medical services, including the school medical service, and now, at one stroke, the Council had taken control of a vast and comprehensive series of hospitals ranging from general hospitals and mental institutions to children's hospitals and convalescent homes.

Altogether, 74 hospitals had come under the control of the L.C.C. The Municipal Hospitals were able to provide 43,284 beds while the Voluntary Hospitals pro-

A Municipal Health Service

vided 13,319 beds. Approximately 76 per cent. of the hospital accommodation in London was now provided by the Municipal Services. It would be a very dull imagination which was not captured by the prospect of providing London with a great Municipal Health Service which equalled both the needs and the opportunity.

It is difficult to say what the Municipal Reformers might have made of this opportunity. The hospitals were transferred to the Council on the 1st April 1930, and they might justly claim that time was required for a complete survey of this immense new service. Then, as we have seen, the Municipal Reformers had responded to the panic appeals for " economy " and there was little money available for modernising and equipping the hospitals. Certainly, very little progress had been made by the time Labour came to power at County Hall.

Here is a summary of the position as Labour found it on taking power in March 1934.

1. The standard of accommodation and equipment of the municipal hospitals were, in many cases, highly unsatisfactory, to say the least. There were hospitals which were appallingly dilapidated—wards with the walls unplastered and the floors worn out.

2. Few of the hospitals had modern facilities for surgical treatment, and in many cases the X-ray, dental and pathological departments were inadequate.

3. The boiler-houses, engine-rooms, kitchens and laundries of many hospitals were inefficient or obsolete.

4. The accommodation for special types of patients was entirely inadequate. In particular, maternity cases and those suffering from incipient mental diseases were very poorly provided for and isolation accommodation was sadly deficient.

5. The standards of diet for patients and the staff catering arrangements were far from satisfactory.

6. The numbers of doctors and nurses were a long way below the standard required to give efficient service.

It was obvious that a great deal of work had to be done before an efficient and comprehensive Municipal Health Service could be erected on these foundations. An immense programme of re-equipping, modernising and, where necessary, re-building the hospitals would have to be carried out. The hospitals, many of them already seriously overcrowded, could not be closed down while the work of reconstruction was carried out, and an exhaustive schedule was prepared of the work to be done which provided for the modernising and re-equipping of the hospitals, ward by ward, block by block, until in some cases the entire hospital had been transformed, internally at any rate, beyond recognition.

An important aspect of Labour's plan of development was that the hospitals should be completely removed from the control of the Poor Law. Under the scheme drawn up by the Tory Council, although the hospitals were administered by the Central Health Committee, they were still dealt with as Poor Law services, and their accounts came under the heading of Public Assistance. This was far more than a mere technical point. The Ministry of Health had to be consulted with regard to the detailed administration of all the Poor Law services, and to continue to operate the hospitals under the Poor Law would limit the Council's power to deal swiftly with the situation. On the other hand, once the hospitals were completely transferred to the public health services, the Ministry had only to be consulted when it was proposed to borrow money for capital expenditure.

There was also another consideration of some importance. So long as the hospitals remained under the Poor Law, everyone who came to them for treatment became technically a " poor person ", and the normal method of

A Municipal Health Service 139

securing admission to the hospitals was by means of the Relieving Officer. Public confidence could never be completely established in a service which was so obviously part of the notorious Poor Law system.

This situation was swiftly changed by the Labour Council. Within a short space of time all the Council's hospitals—general, special and mental—were entirely removed from the atmosphere and control of the Poor Law. It was with some satisfaction that Herbert Morrison was able to inform the Council that the only way a relieving officer could enter an L.C.C. hospital was by becoming a patient.

With the removal of the municipal hospitals from the Poor Law, the administrative distinctions between the different sorts of hospitals could also be removed, and a new classification and grouping of the hospitals became possible. There was general agreement among medical experts that the ideal hospital unit was the large general hospital of not more than 1,000 or at the very most 1,200 beds built on the pavilion system with ward blocks completely separated or united only by covered corridors. A unit up to this size had the advantage that it could be efficiently administered by one medical or lay superintendent, and it could contain wards for medical, surgical and maternity cases to meet the general needs of the people within its area. It could provide an efficient out-patients department, and would be the centre for the ante-natal, dental, school medical and midwifery services of the district. It was the intention of the Labour Council to provide this comprehensive and efficient range of services through each of the general hospitals as rapidly as the equipment was made available and the work of reconstruction could be pushed ahead.

There was no intention, however, that each of these large general hospitals should carry on their work in isolation. It was impossible for a hospital of even 1,200 beds to provide the best facilities for the diagnosis and treatment of every type of disease. While all the ordinary medical, surgical and maternity cases were, therefore, admitted to the nearest general hospital, these hospitals were themselves grouped so that the less common complaints, especially those requiring the skill of specialised doctors or the use of complicated apparatus, were transferred to special units attached to one of the general hospitals. In this way the greatest degree of specialised skill and the resources of costly apparatus could be concentrated on the needs of special classes of patients.

Around this system of grouping the Council rapidly built up a full range of specialist units, which served the needs of the whole metropolitan area. For example, the Lambeth Hospital became the centre for the treatment of cancer, using the full scope of the latest X-ray and radium therapy methods of treatment. St. James's Hospital, Fulham, developed an extensive plastic surgery unit ; special clinics for diabetics were opened at St. George-in-the-East and St. Peter's hospital : an important unit for the treatment of all forms of rheumatism was attached to St. Stephen's Hospital ; thoracic surgery was mainly carried out at St. Mary Abbots, and Queen Mary's Hospital, Carshalton, became probably the world's foremost hospital for the treatment of crippled children.

Arising from this grouping of the hospitals and the development of the specialist units came vastly extended opportunities for the investigation of the innumerable problems associated with health and disease. Full-time consultant specialists were appointed to take charge of each unit, supported by teams of highly qualified specialist assistants, and steps were taken to ensure that all the available time of these specialists was not occupied with

A Municipal Health Service

routine work. The result has been that during the past ten years many important discoveries in medical treatment have been made by workers in the L.C.C. hospitals. It is continually stated by those who oppose any form of National or Municipal Health Services that the result would be to " stifle the spirit of research and slow down medical progress ". The experience of the Municipal Hospitals in London has provided a swift and complete answer to that hoary calumny. Each year in the supplement to the Report on the L.C.C. Hospital Services there is published a long list of the original achievements in medical and surgical research, the development of new techniques, the fresh advances towards the conquest of sickness and disease which have been carried out by the doctors, surgeons, physicists, radiologists and the other medical technicians who work in the special units and general hospitals of the London County Council. The great Municipal Health Service of the metropolis provided the scope, the opportunity and the resources for medical research on a scale which enabled rapid progress to be made in many fields.

But we are running somewhat ahead of the account. Before this stage was reached the hospitals had to be taken out of the shadow of the Poor Law, and the Hospitals and Medical Services Committee under the Chairmanship of Dr. Somerville Hastings, M.P., and with Dan Frankel, as Vice-Chairman, had to remedy many deficiencies, overcome many obstacles and solve some very intractable problems before the hospitals and their allied services were co-ordinated and grouped into an efficient municipal health service.

It is not possible within the limits of this brief survey to give anything like a full account of the improvements in accommodation and in scientific and medical equipment which were introduced into the municipal hospitals.

The full story fills many pages of the reports of the Hospitals and Medical Services Committee. It is only possible here to record some of the more important features of that immense programme of re-construction and re-equipment.

The appallingly dilapidated condition of many of the hospitals made it necessary to carry out several major building schemes. The North-Eastern Hospital at Tottenham, for example, was reconstructed and modernised at a cost of £214,000. The Heatherwood Hospital at Ascot was enlarged at an expenditure of £72,000. The Lambeth Hospital was completely modernised at a cost of £300,000, and at Hackney £250,000 was spent in bringing buildings and equipment up to date. The construction of new ward blocks at Paddington and Mile End cost £52,000 and £73,000 respectively. Other new ward blocks were built at Hammersmith, St. Matthew's, St. Nicholas's, and special isolation accommodation was built for the hospitals at Shooters, Dartford and at New Cross. That is a brief extract from a long catalogue of building, reconstruction and re-equipping which was pressed ahead at increasing speed. Briefly, within three years of Labour coming to power, decisions had been taken to enlarge, modernise and re-equip no less than thirty-seven hospitals.

As we have seen, it was the policy of the Council to group the hospitals for the purpose, among other things, of establishing special clinics and specialist units at many of the general hospitals. But in a comprehensive scheme for a public health service these special units and the hospitals themselves had to be served by special laboratories and other supplementary medical services. For example, a new pathological laboratory was built at Hampstead to serve the Northern Group of Hospitals, and another large group pathological laboratory was

A Municipal Health Service

built at Lambeth. To meet the requirements of all the hospitals a great serum institute was built at Carshalton at a cost of £116,000. The provisions for convalescent treatment were also rapidly extended to serve the requirements of the hospitals.

It had not been the practice of the Poor Law infirmaries to provide an out-patient service. New accommodation was provided at most of the general hospitals to remedy this shortcoming. Casualty and emergency cases, hospital and other cases requiring after-care, antenatal and post-natal cases were treated at the rapidly growing out-patient departments of the Council's hospitals. To an increasing extent the hospitals were able to provide a comprehensive medical service to the surrounding community.

Inside the hospitals the wards were completely transformed. The unplastered walls, the heavy beamed ceilings and narrow windows gave place to wards full of sunlight and air. Colours invaded the formerly drab and monotonous surroundings. Glass and polished chrome gave a new perspective to the wards. Chintz bed coverings, well-designed furniture and flowers from the L.C.C. parks introduced a new atmosphere of comfort and cheerfulness. Medical science recognises the value of the psychological factor in the treatment of sickness, and these new, colourful amenities, by their influence on the mental attitudes of the patients, became important elements in the process of treatment.

In carrying out this immense programme of renovation and rebuilding the requirements of the medical and nursing staffs were not overlooked. The buildings and equipment of many of the nurses' Homes were as dilapidated as the hospitals themselves. These nurses' homes were renovated and equipped with modern furniture and conveniences. By the beginning of 1938, eleven nurses' homes had been completely modernised, and decisions had been taken to press ahead with similar improvements at another fourteen homes. In addition to this work of renovation, completely new nurses' homes had to be built to accommodate the large increase in nursing staff required to operate the hospitals efficiently. A new home was built at Hackney at a cost of £98,000, and further new homes were erected at Colindale, Grove Park, Brentwood, Islington and Hammersmith.

The accommodation for the medical and domestic staff was similarly improved. New dispensaries were built and comfortable waiting-rooms constructed for those who had to spend long and anxious hours in attendance on relatives and friends.

The process of reconstruction was carried on in places which the average patient never sees, but whose efficiency contributed to the progress and comfort of every patient in the hospital. Kitchens were modernised and equipped with up-to-date cooking facilities. New boiler-houses were constructed, old plant was modernised and additional laundry equipment provided at many of the hospitals.

This short summary will give some impression of the extensive programme of building, modernising and re-equipping which was carried out by the Labour Council in the five years between April 1934 and the outbreak of war in 1939. There were, however, other urgent improvements needed in the hospitals which could be more swiftly carried out.

In 1934 the shortage of medical and nursing staff in the hospitals was acute. Doctors and nurses were compelled to work long and unreasonable hours, and this lack of medical and nursing staff, in turn, seriously affected the welfare and comfort of the patients. Immediate steps were taken to remedy this situation.

A Municipal Health Service 145

Within two months of taking office, the Labour Council had created 125 new supervisory nursing positions in the hospitals, and in July of the same year 37 additional doctors were appointed to the staff. Twelve months later the nursing staff at the 27 general hospitals had been increased by 695, and the number of women orderlies had grown from 124 to 550. Further substantial increases of nursing and medical staff were made from time to time in order to keep pace with the expanding scope of the hospital services. The doctors were in a position to give the necessary individual attention to their patients and a great burden of unnecessary work was lifted from the shoulders of the nurses.

In July 1935 the hours of duty of both the day and night nursing staff were reduced from up to 66 hours to a uniform 54 hours a week. In May 1938 the decision was taken to further reduce the hours by the adoption of the 96-hour fortnight. These reductions in working hours were also extended to the women orderlies.

The petty restrictions which had confined the freedom of the nurses in their hours off duty were swept away. The nurses could smoke in their bedrooms, they were given much wider freedom to spend their free time outside the hospitals, recreation rooms and gymnasia were provided for their use and they were able to stay at nurses' homes attached to the country and seaside hospitals. In the municipal hospitals nursing lost many of its worst restrictions and began to secure the amenities of a profession.

Within three years the " Poor Law Infirmaries " had been transformed from their stagnant condition into modern hospitals equipped with all the skill and resources required to undertake the efficient diagnosis and treatment of sickness and disease. These general hospitals, in turn, were supported by modern pathological laboratories, institutes for the manufacture of special antitoxins and sera, centres for advanced radium and X-ray treatment, and special hospital units under the care of leading London specialists in particular branches of medicine, surgery and obstetrics. A patient in an L.C.C. hospital was in a position to secure the most up-to-date treatment which specialist skill and medical science could provide. It was an object lesson in what could be accomplished for the public health by a progressive authority which could command the enthusiasm of its Health Committee, secure the requisite ability for direction and provide the necessary funds for development.

So far we have dealt mainly with the general hospitals for the acute and chronic cases which were taken over from the Boards of Guardians. In addition to these, however, the Council had also taken over the special hospital service of the Metropolitan Asylums Board, consisting of eighteen hospitals for infectious diseases, nine hospitals for tuberculosis and five children's hospitals. The treatment of infectious disease in London—possibly for reasons which have already been described—had been much better developed than was the case for less contagious complaints, and the Labour Council did not have to face the same problems of differing conditions which had made the re-organisation and renovation of the general hospitals such a serious and urgent task. Even in these hospitals, however, a great deal was done to bring them completely up to modern standards of accommodation and equipment.

The isolation accommodation was rapidly extended to avoid any possibility of " cross-infection " between cases. Very extensive improvements were carried out at the children's hospitals. Additional laboratories were provided and the central heating and kitchen equipment improved. Specialised units were also devel-

A Municipal Health Service

oped for each group of special hospitals to carry out research and treatment of particular complaints. For example, at the North-Eastern Hospital a special department was developed for treating chronic carriers of diphtheria, and Miss Kenny, the Australian nurse who had demonstrated a new method of treating infantile paralysis, was invited to establish a special clinic at the Queen Mary's Hospital for Children at Carshalton.

The facilities for the treatment of tuberculosis were very greatly improved. Additional accommodation was provided at the tuberculosis hospitals and sanatoria so that there should not be any appreciable waiting time before a patient was able to commence treatment. The sanatoria were equipped with new balconies to provide extended open-air treatment. An important decision of the Council was that all contributions towards the cost of residential treatment of tuberculosis should be abolished on the grounds that tuberculous patients on leaving the sanatoria would almost invariably need all their financial resources to provide nourishing food and other comforts necessary to resist the disease. Greater facilities were provided for the after-care of patients, and the children of tuberculous parents were given the opportunity of going to special open-air nursery schools at the seaside and in the country.

The next chapter will describe some of the extensions of the School Medical Services. There are, however, many other aspects of the development of the public health services under the Labour Council which we cannot even touch upon with the present limits. The improvements in the medical relief stations, the improved methods of treatment and training for the blind, the special clinics and hospitals for the epilectics, the development of psychiatric out-patients clinics with trained social workers, the institution of the hospital almoner system, and the extension of the system of convalescent treatment. All these, and many other, important contributions to the health of the metropolis are unfortunately beyond the scope of the present volume.

There is one very important development, however, which cannot be passed swiftly over—the maternity services. Under the Labour Council these maternity services were, literally, transformed beyond recognition. Conditions inside the maternity wards had been so unsatisfactory that it was only poverty or an extreme emergency which could persuade a London mother to enter the bleak and shabby wards of the " Poor Law Hospital and Institution." But within a few years the change which had come over the attitude of London mothers to this aspect of the Council's health services was remarkably complete.

The shabby maternity wards were completely modernised as part of the general scheme of hospital reconstruction. The obstetrical equipment was brought up to the best modern standards, and under a special scheme the expectant mother was provided with the services of some of the best obstetricians and gynaecologists in London.

The Council also organised an emergency service to deal with maternity patients who could not be moved to hospital without risk. In the case of urgent need, specialist attention and expert nursing care was made available to the mother in her own home. At every hour of the day and night this expert " Flying Squad " was ready to bring skilled assistance to any London mother who might require it.

In addition to this emergency service, the Council organised a Home Midwifery and Maternity Nursing Service. Before the war over 10,000 mothers every year were receiving midwifery and nursing attention at their homes.

A Municipal Health Service 149

The following figures show the increasing extent to which the new maternity services were used by mothers of London within the short period of a few years.

Maternity Services	1932	1937
Confinements in L.C.C. hospitals	11,239	19,614
Ante-natal attendances in out-patient clinics	48,618	132,270
Maternal death-rate per 1,000 births	7·2	2·49

The decline in the maternal death-rate alone is evidence of the improved quality and standard of the maternity hospital services.

Another vast field of public health which came under the Labour Council's control was the twenty-one mental hospitals with nearly 34,000 patients. At most of these hospitals structural changes comparable to those effected at the general hospitals were carried out. Up to the outbreak of war no less than £1,000,000 were spent in bringing the standards of accommodation and equipment into line with modern requirements. Even more important than these structural changes was the humanising influence which was promoted as a deliberate policy in all the mental hospitals. It has been undeniably proved that in the dark and uncertain realms of mental disorder and mental deficiency, humanity and science must walk hand in hand. The dress of the male and female patients was completely modernised to conform to ordinary civilian standards. The heavy crockery formerly in use was superseded by vitrified crockery similar to that used by wealthy patients. Canteens were opened at all the large hospitals to provide toilet preparations, sweets, tobacco and other small sundries. The cinema and radio brightened the lives and improved the mental outlook of thousands of patients. To the fullest possible degree, the attempt was made to make the conditions inside the mental hospitals conform to the normal usages and standards of the outside world.

Many new forms of treatment have been initiated and developed in the Council's mental hospitals since 1934. In particular, mention must be made of the introduction of insulin and electric shock therapy. There are strong grounds for anticipating that the development of these techniques will push open the door to normal life and sanity for many people who have hitherto been regarded as incurable. Research has also been carried out with regard to a delicate brain operation—pre-frontal leucotomy—which may also provide the door to normal living for another large group of patients. Not even the most uncompromising opponent of municipal enterprise could suggest that in this field the municipal health service had a " stultifying influence on the progress of medical research." The work of the Council's mental hospitals has received world-wide recognition.

In the case of patients who are discharged from the mental hospitals the care does not stop short at the hospital doors. In 1935 arrangements were made to provide vocational training for patients who, on leaving the hospital after successful treatment, required an opportunity to fit themselves for some new kind of work less exacting than their former jobs, which, by their monotony or strain, may have contributed to their breakdown. This arrangement has lead to very encouraging results. In many ways the skill and resources which have been devoted to the intractable problems of mental disorder and deficiency in the Council's hospitals are yielding results which may prove of incalculable benefit to thousands of people in Britain, and throughout the world.

The wideness of the field over which the Council's medical services extend, and the immense raising of the standards of equipment and specialist skill, have brought them to the forefront as training-grounds for the medical profession. The majority of the general and special hospitals provide instruction for medical undergraduates. Most notable of all, the Council, in co-operation with the Ministry of Health and the University of London, in 1935 established a post-graduate medical school at the Hammersmith Hospital, where general medical practitioners could secure knowledge of the most recent advances in medical science. This school still remains the first school devoted solely to the education of medical graduates.

Within five years the dilapidated " Poor Law Institutions " of London had been transformed into modern, well-equipped hospitals with all their ancillary services. It is an achievement which has already left its imprint on thousands of lives. A new confidence has been created among Londoners in their municipal hospitals. Londoners know that within their wards and special units, should they ever need it, is the very best that medical science and skill can provide.

In September 1939 the great municipal hospital system of London faced the emergencies of war, equipped and prepared for any task which might come to them.

CHAPTER VIII

PROGRESS IN EDUCATION

THERE could be no doubt about Labour's attitude to education in London. It had been made evident in the proposals of the Labour members of the Education Committee and in the debates which were initiated in the Council Chamber. Everyone who had any interest in London's education services knew that Labour in power at County Hall meant a new era in the history of Education in London.

The responsibility for the quality and efficiency of the education services in London was not a burden to be carried lightly. In round figures there were over 414,000 children in 900 elementary schools; 29,000 children in 89 central schools and 34,000 in 79 secondary schools; over 10,000 children in nearly a hundred special schools for sick and handicapped children; 1,000 in nursery schools, and more than 276,000 people of all ages who looked to the L.C.C. for continued and technical education. In short, over three-quarters of a million minds were in the keeping of the L.C.C. education services.

The new Education Committee began its task with its resources reduced by the effects of the National Economy Act passed in 1931, when the " National " Government had forced considerable economies on the whole range of the social services. Before 1931 the expenditure on London's education services had been shared almost equally by the Government and the Council. The National Economy Act, which remained in force long after the pretext for its imposition had disappeared, had altered the balance of contributions so that the Government now bore only approximately 37 per cent. of the

Progress in Education

cost, placing an increased burden of more than £1,000,000 a year on the Council.

A million pounds can go a very long way when applied to education. It could, for example, pay the salaries of several thousand additional teachers, or provide 22,000 more London children with the benefits of secondary and higher education. It would build a score of new schools and equip them with all the latest resources of education. On the other hand, a deficit of this magnitude could become a deadening handicap in the whole range of the education services. By 1937 the Government had " saved " over £7,000,000 at the expense of London's children. Under other circumstances this deficit might have reduced the quality of the education of a whole generation of London's children.

The Government created " deficit " was serious, but even more serious was the situation revealed by the Education Committee's survey of the entire education services.

More than one hundred and fifty elementary schools urgently required re-conditioning or completely rebuilding. Thousands of children were still spending their school hours in dark and often unhealthy classrooms. In winter, the only illumination of these dark and drab surroundings was often the flickering glare of an old-fashioned gas-burner. The equipment of all the schools —elementary, central and secondary—fell a long way behind modern requirements. Science laboratories, gymnasia, equipment for teaching handicrafts were inadequate or totally lacking in many districts. Incredible as it may seem, there were still a very large number of schools in London in which the sanitary accommodation remained the primitive " open trough " system.

The provision of school buildings had fallen behind housing developments in London. Many children were compelled to make long and fatiguing journeys to school. New elementary, central and secondary schools were urgently needed to meet the changed location and balance of the population. The position of many of the technical institutes and special schools was not much better. Many of the buildings and a lot of the equipment were utterly inadequate to meet the demands made on them.

Nor was that all in the catalogue of deficiencies. As a matter of foremost urgency it was necessary to reduce the serious overcrowding in many of the infants' and elementary schools. Many of the infant classes had attendance rolls as high as 53. The average number of children per teacher in the classes of the elementary and central schools was 31. This was the total average figure which concealed still more gravely overcrowded classes in several districts. Effective education cannot even begin when teachers are carrying the burden of overcrowded classes.

The facilities for secondary and higher education were also a long way behind the needs of London's children. There was serious evidence that the existing income limits for the award of Junior County exhibitions and other scholarships were shutting out many brilliant children from the opportunities for higher education.

Finally, the school welfare and medical services were most obviously in need of urgent extensions. The school medical and dental services, if they were to fulfil their task, required to be made more frequent in their application and much more comprehensive in their scope. There was an urgent need for further special clinics and schools for sick and handicapped children. The school feeding arrangements were patently inadequate. There was, in fact, a most evident necessity for a complete overhaul and extension of the school medical, dental and special services.

Progress in Education

This catalogue of deficiencies in school services represented the leeway which the new Education Committee had to make up. It must also be remembered that the Committee had to move within the rigid framework of the powers conferred on the L.C.C. as an education authority. No matter how generous its intentions, no matter how urgent the need, the Committee could not move a fraction beyond the limits laid down by Parliament. It could not, for example, by itself, raise the school-leaving age to 15, or decide to abolish the fees charged in secondary schools—two necessary reforms which the Labour Party had long beem demanding. The Committee could not set out to make London a Utopia of modern education. But it could set out to infuse a new sense of ideals and purpose into the machinery of the education services. It could remedy the grave deficiencies in buildings, equipment and special services. It could push still further open the gates of educational opportunity for every child in London. In short, the London Education Committee could set itself the task of bringing the London school services into line with modern educational practices and requirements. And that, as we shall see, was in itself no small achievement.

There was most obviously need for many urgent reforms and improvements in the education services. But education is a field where even the strongest sense of urgency must be tempered with a necessary expediency. Progress in education should not be abrupt and spasmodic. The advance towards a new objective in educational policy should always be made without appearing to break rudely open the existing curriculum, or introducing sudden and disturbing changes in the school lives of the children. Teachers should know a long time in advance of any impending alterations so that the necessary changes may be made in school life with the minimum of disturbance. In the best pedagogics there is no room for swift innovation. In education the best revolutions are always the least perceptible. It should be said of any important change in school life that, like Topsy, it " just growed ".

It was essential, then, that the necessary changes in and improvements to the education services should be conceived as part of an adequate long term development and reform. The proposals of the Education Committee were, therefore, based on a series of " Three-Year Programmes ". Following a comprehensive survey of all the education services, the Labour Council adopted the first of its famous " Three-Year Programmes " in February 1935. This programme aimed at a balanced advance over the whole field of London's education services. The second " Three-Year Programme ", that for 1938-41, was shattered before completion by the outbreak of war.

In terms of new building and reconstruction the following figures convey some impression of the extent of the programme which was carried out in less than four years.

New Elementary Schools and enlargements	30
New Central Schools	7
New Scondary Schools	5
Elementary Schools modernised	150
Secondary Schools modernised	20
New Technical Institutes	4
Technical Institutes modernised	6
New Nursery Schools	7
New Special Schools	7
New Open Air Schools	7
New Training Colleges	1

That this programme of new building and reconstruction had to be carried out at a time when the school population of London was actually shrinking is abundant evidence of the extent to which the provision of schools and institutes had fallen behind the requirements of the metropolis.

The standards of planning for the new schools were completely revised, giving larger, well-lit classrooms, hot water in every cloakroom, better facilities for teaching handicrafts, domestic and science subjects ; libraries, gymnasia and shower-baths were incorporated in the plans. Many of the older schools were completely reconditioned and replanned. Dark, drab classrooms, " open-trough sanitation ", and flickering gas-jets gave place to wide, airy classrooms, hot- and cold-water services, medical inspection rooms and the provision of central assembly halls. The standard laid down for the public schools of London provided many of the facilities and amenities which had hitherto been reserved for the children at the much more exclusive sort of " Public Schools ".

New and improved furniture was introduced into the schools. The educational facilities provided by books, picture and gramophone records were considerably extended. The number of epidiascopes was increased from a few dozen to more than two hundred instruments. In 1934 a few schools were supplied with radio equipment through the kindness of a voluntary organisation ; at the outbreak of war nearly every school in London had been completely equipped with its radiogram and other wireless apparatus. In 1935 it was decided that the schools should be equipped with cinema projectors, and by 1938 130 projectors were in use in the schools supported by a Film Library consisting of many hundred films. Special rooms were equipped with modern apparatus for the teaching of geography and history. The equipment of the school laboratories was brought completely up to date. At the outbreak of war the Labour Council was spending

£500,000 a year on books and educational equipment for the schools.

This new equipment and the improved facilities had their effects on the quality of education provided in the schools. The lessons could be made more complete, more vivid and arresting, without diminishing in any way that stimulus to mental effort and concentration which must remain the basis of a system which builds both mind and character.

Another development which had an important effect on the quality of education in the elementary schools was the improvements which were introduced into the Junior County Scholarships system. These scholarships were the passports from the elementary schools to six years' higher education in an approved secondary school, and they were awarded to children at 11 years on the basis of a written competitive examination. For children of working-class parents these scholarships meant a long period of anxious cramming and preparation. Furthermore, the prospect of these examinations had largely dominated the subjects and methods of teaching in the primary schools.

The Labour Party on the L.C.C. were convinced, as were most modern educationists, that the system whereby a child's opportunity for higher education depended on a single arbitrary examination, mainly in arithmetic and English, should be abolished, and that any required educational test should be based on the whole of a child's school record and general ability. Any such change, however, had to await the general recasting of the whole educational system. In the meantime, the Education Committee gave every encouragement to the school inspectors to set new standards in the scholarship examinations. A common-sense interpretation of the questions became more important than the ability to assimilate a

Progress in Education

mass of facts and figures. A large amount of arithmetic was cut out of the examination and far more emphasis was placed on a general paper framed to test the ability of the child. These new standards had their effects right throughout the primary schools. The whole bias of the education was altered. The tendency to overpress the children to prepare for examinations was eliminated. The children were no longer burdened with hours of dull cramming. A great deal of the drudgery—and anxiety—of elementary education disappeared.

It was important that the scholarship system, while it was still retained, should provide a fair test of ability. And equally important was the need to ensure that every child who could benefit from higher education should not be denied the opportunity because there were too few places available. The Labour Council brought continual pressure to bear on the Board of Education to secure the required sanction to increase the number of scholarships and exhibitions available for London children with considerable success. In 1930 the number of free places available in the secondary schools was 37 per cent. of the total. By 1938 over 53 per cent. of the children in the secondary schools were admitted free. The further extension of the number of scholarships was interrupted, like so many other educational projects, by the outbreak of war.

Other steps were taken to ensure that no child in London should be deprived of the opportunity for higher education through lack of means. The income limits of parents of children receiving scholarships were raised. The amount of money available for school journeys was substantially increased, and, in 1938, it was decided that, where necessary, pupils in secondary schools should be assisted by grants towards the provision of meals and outfits.

Better facilities and wider opportunities were provided for the children of London. But a child who is undernourished cannot get the full benefit of any system of education, and in the years before the war, undernourishment was the great menace which touched the lives of thousands of schoolchildren.

From the start of its work, the Education Committee was fully aware that its work to improve the facilities and opportunities for education in London could be completely stultified by the slow handicap imposed by undernourishment. Five special Nutrition Centres were established by the Council at which children could be examined by physicians trained to detect the often latent effects of undernourishment in children. Where children were found to be having wrong or insufficient food, the parents were informed, and the children given nourishing food through the school feeding organisation, together with any necessary vitamin preparations and special medicines.

The system of medical inspection in the schools was overhauled and radically improved. Arrangements were made for the children to receive far more regular and frequent medical and dental inspection. Defects which might otherwise have left a legacy of ill-health were more promptly detected and put right.

Seven additional Special Schools, including two new residential schools, were opened for those whose education had to be adapted to a more prolonged mental or physical handicap. Special centres were opened for the treatment of children who stammered, and over 800 beds were provided in the Council's hospitals for the treatment of rheumatic children, while at the same time making special arrangements to ensure that their education went forward.

The facilities for sport and recreation were rapidly expanded. Wherever the cramped sprawl of London

Progress in Education 161

made it possible, land adjoining the schools was purchased in order to extend the size of the playgrounds. The planless growth of London had long ago swallowed up the green spaces which could have provided playgrounds and sports fields for the children, so the Labour Council began to create an " Educational Green Belt " for the schools of London. About 700 acres of open spaces, parks, downs and woodlands, were acquired outside London for playing fields to which all children over 10 could be taken out one day a week. There, amid country surroundings, in lightly constructed classrooms, they could play games, learn the secrets of the countryside and carry on their education in surroundings very different from those of the congested London districts from whence they had come.

So much for the elementary, special and secondary schools. But there was another vast field of education into which the Council also introduced many improvements and reforms. " Technical and Continued Education " describes the further education provided in nearly 250 institutes of various kinds, comprising polytechnics, technical and trade schools, schools of art, day continuation schools and evening institutes for which the Council was also responsible.

The efficiency of several hundred skilled trades, from printing, bookbinding and leatherwork to technical optics, furnishing and carriage building, depended on the standards and facilities provided in the technical and trade institutes. The training of the skilled personnel of commerce and the distributive trades rested on the polytechnics and evening institutes. But, in 1934, the first survey of this immensely important field of continued education revealed the now familiar account of deficiencies and defects. Many of these institutes were handicapped by inadequate accommodation and a serious lack of equipment. In this sphere, too, the Education Committee had to carry out an extensive programme of building, modernisation and re-equipment.

The St. Martin's School of Art and the Technical Institute for the Distributive Trades were rehoused in a new building in Charing Cross Road at a cost of £86,000. The City Literary Institute was accommodated in a splendid new building costing £56,000 and the Shoreditch Technical Institute for Women was also provided with new premises. It cost £35,000 to provide the Woolwich Polytechnic with the necessary new accommodation for its students, and over £11,000 was spent in bringing the Northampton Polytechnic up to date. Ten of the existing polytechnics and technical institutes were enlarged, and sites had been purchased and building work actually begun at the outbreak of war on extensions for two more institutes. At nearly all of the institutes the machinery and equipment needed modernising and extending. The courses at many of the institutes were extended to cover new technical and professional developments. Courses were commenced, for example, in civil aviation and television.

The Council also established a fund to develop physical training and recreation among its great army of technical and part-time students. A camp site was set aside at Chigwell to provide a permanent centre with accommodation, dining and recreational facilities.

A full account of the educational progress and innovation in London during the years before the war is beyond the scope of this book. This brief sketch will convey, however, some impression of the work which was done by the Labour Council to widen the educational opportunities in the thousand schools and institutes of London, and to promote the welfare and happiness of all who had recourse to them.

CHAPTER IX

PEACE AND PROGRESS

LONDON is the greatest monument on earth to the virtues of free enterprise. The uncontrolled rights of the landowners to develop their land for their own profit had created the maze of congested streets, the ugly sprawling growth of the slums, the factories which had turned residential districts into insanitary areas, and had raised the value of the land to such a fantastic level that it had become beyond the powers of the County Council to straighten out the appalling muddle of the metropolis. You cannot afford to do much street widening at the rate of a million pounds a mile. Furthermore, when improvements were carried out, the result was to add to the value of the surrounding property and so make the next improvement more costly and more difficult. There is now only one method of cutting the vast, complicated Gorgon's knot of London's planning difficulties—to secure the public ownership of the land on which this gigantic conurbation has been built.

But even within the limits of its existing powers and resources the Labour Council in London, in the years before the war, did a great deal to remedy the worst aspects of the uncontrolled development of the metropolis.

As long ago as 1909 the London County Council had acquired powers under the Town Planning Act, 1909, to control the use of land and for fixing the density of building. But with the Tory Councils these powers rested in abeyance. The unregulated development of London by the landowners and the speculators continued at the same frantic pace.

It was not until 1924 that the first timid approach was

made to the vast problem, when twenty acres of open spaces were included in the first town-planning resolution to be passed for the metropolis. It was the gesture of a purblind Canute—already the vast unregulated tide of bricks and mortar had flowed like twisted lava across nearly the whole of the County of London.

In the following years, under the energetic pressure of the Labour Party on the Council, the Municipal Reformers were compelled to take action to protect some of the more conspicuous amenities of London. The space around Westminster Abbey, for example, was saved from being swallowed in a building scheme. By 1934 the piebald patches of sixteen small schemes had been applied to the vast face of London.

In March 1934, therefore, the problem of making the growth of London conform to some sort of ordered plan was not the least of the many vast problems which confronted the Labour Council. Between March and June 1934 the whole question was examined in all its complicated details by the Town Planning Committee. To lay the guiding hand of town planning on the remaining 52,000 acres of intensely developed and ever-changing property, to attempt after centuries of unregulated growth to fit the vast huddle of the metropolis into an ordered plan for its growth and community life, was one of the most formidable projects which ever confronted a local authority. But that was the bold decision which the Town Planning Committee recommended to the Council, and which the Council, in turn, accepted.

The Town Planning Committee had some foreknowledge of the immense task they were attempting. The twenty-eight Metropolitan Boroughs were asked to prepare planning proposals for their areas in outline, while the Town Planning Committee prepared a plan for the County generally on the broadest lines. Consultations

Peace and Progress

with the Borough Councils followed on both sets of plans, and the Committee then prepared a draft scheme for the Council, which was advertised to set in motion a procedure similar to that described in some detail in the chapter on slum clearance.

The opposition to the proposal for bringing London under planning control was immediate and formidable. Large and small landlords were banded together into a determined opposition to any restrictions being placed on their rights to develop their properties in accordance with their private interests. The public enquiry into their complaints was begun in January 1935, and lasted for three weeks ; twenty-four counsel and a great array of expert witnesses appeared to argue on the great issues involved. One fact became abundantly clear during the course of that enquiry—to allow the future growth of the metropolis to be determined by unregulated whims of the private landowners would be to make London into a " disaster for all its inhabitants ". London was a city already perilously near to social suffocation through the planless haste of its development. Another fact began to emerge, too, at an early state in the enquiry. As the Council's proposals were unfolded in detail it became evident that in time London would be a far better developed city under planning than it would be if left unregulated. The value of the property within the planned area would naturally increase. Among many of the larger landowners the frantic note in their opposition began to die down as this fact became patent. It is an unescapable fact that, under present circumstances, almost every improvement in the life of a community must inevitably add to the increments of the landowners.

The draft scheme of the Council was finally approved by the Ministry of Health, except for the Inns of Court, which were regarded as " static areas " not likely to be developed within any measurable space of time. After centuries of haphazard development, the growth of London had henceforth to conform to some extent to the needs of its inhabitants. This does not mean that the Council had powers to make the crooked straight. The existing properties were not affected. The need for conforming to the plan would only arise when the existing property was demolished and a new one was to be erected in its place. The new building had then to meet the requirements of the planning authority. It is obvious, therefore, that while bringing London under planning control would halt the spread of further abuses, it could not sweep away the mass of bad building and congested streets, or make London within an appreciable time a much better and convenient place to live in.

The Bressey Report, published in 1937, estimated that an expenditure of £250,000,000 would be required to provide Greater London with a system of highways adequate for its needs. That was for highways alone. In a previous chapter we have already looked at the cost of land in London. It is obvious that under the existing system of land ownership and compensation—which have in no way been substantially modified by wartime legislation—it was beyond the resources of the Council to straighten out the fantastic muddle of the metropolis.

None the less, the Labour Council decided to make a bold attempt to remedy some of the worst defects in the haphazard layout of the capital. London's streets are not paved with gold, but millions of pounds are lost in the streets of London every year. There were many points where the dense flow of London's peace-time traffic was suddenly strangulated by narrowing streets or halted by the congealing influence of cross-traffic points.

Plans were made for many large-scale improvements in

London's traffic routes. A series of new arterial roads were planned for by-passing the congested central areas and linking up the cross traffic with new circular roads on the outskirts of London. Legislation was secured, jointly with the Middlesex County Council, to link up Cromwell Road by a new arterial road with the Great West Road, the total cost of this scheme being £2,500,000. Another important arterial development put under way was the Western Avenue extension which provided for Marylebone Road to be extended to Edgware Road, and for a new road to be constructed from Wood Lane to Latimer Road at a cost of over a million pounds. Further important improvements were carried out on the construction of the South Circular Road and the Wandsworth High Street by-pass.

In addition to the construction of new main and arterial roads, many important traffic routes were widened and improved. In one year alone, 1937, widening schemes were carried out in such important main routes as Commercial Road, Finchley Road, Horseferry Road, Kensington High Street and York Road, to mention but a few.

In the same year, 1937, the Council obtained the required Parliamentary sanction to widen and improve Notting Hill Gate, so that the narrow congested streets could be extended to carry six lines of easily flowing traffic. The Vauxhall Cross improvement, at a cost of more than £350,000, put an end to the interminable delays of one of the worst traffic junctions in London.

A schedule of the actual improvements carried out in order to expedite the flow of London's traffic would be tediously long. These improvements called for a vast amount of slow and involved negotiations with hundreds of frontagers and landlords. In other countries the need for such vital improvements do not have to wait so patiently on the, often, extortionate exactions of the property owners.

The improvement, however, which possibly attracted most public attention, was the swift and effective way the Labour Council dealt with the problem of Waterloo Bridge.

The story of the Tory Council's handling of Waterloo Bridge is possibly one of the most outstanding examples of vacillation and civic ineptitude in the annals of London's government. About 1923 it was found that Waterloo Bridge was, literally, falling down. The old bridge which had been built to serve the needs of the leisurely, horsedrawn traffic of a hundred years before was breaking up under the grinding pressure of modern traffic. The width, too, was far too congested for the torrent of modern vehicles which sought to cross the river at that point.

The Tory Council hastily underpinned the bridge, and then they leisurely looked at the problem for several years. Then, they tried, very conveniently, to forget all about it, until they were prodded by the Labour Party into having another look at the problem. They drew up some tentative plans for doing something or other. Then they pigeonholed the plans. After more energetic protests they began to plead that it would, after all, be a great pity to " meddle with a masterpiece ", and perhaps the old bridge, with a little propping up, could be made to do. But the spate of traffic which struggled to cross the bridge had greatly increased and the ancient structure was being shaken to its foundations. The masterpiece, if such it was, had become a menace in face of the requirements of a modern community. A temporary bridge had perforce to be erected. The " masterpiece " and the temporary bridge rested side by side. But temporary bridges cannot stay temporary for ever.

Peace and Progress

The situation had become an enigma without any variations.

The action of the Labour Party on taking office was in striking contrast to this policy of fatuous temporisation. An appropriation for the purpose of building a new Bridge was included in the Council's Annual Money Bill which has to be presented to Parliament. But a Tory House of Commons was reluctant to see a Labour Council carry out a project which a Tory Council had failed to achieve. They struck this item out of the Bill.

Faced with this decision, the Labour Council none the less put the work in hand, deciding that the need was so urgent that the cost must be met out of the current rates. There could be no doubt about it. Labour was determined to give London a bridge which modern traffic requirements so plainly and urgently demanded. Faced with the implacable determination of the Labour Council, and with the new bridge well under construction, in 1937, Parliament decided that the Council should receive a grant of 60 per cent. towards the cost of the new bridge. But not a penny towards the cost of pulling the old one down!

Here one can only add that the new bridge was completed in spite of the perils of blitz and buzz-bomb, and that it swiftly made an important contribution to the war effort by speeding up the cross-river traffic of essential war supplies.

The Labour Council acted with equal promptness to preserve for London some of the amenities of the fast-disappearing countryside. Between 1926 and 1933 nearly ten thousand acres of open spaces inside the County were swallowed up by the encroachments of the builder. The natural lungs of London were being choked up. Sites for playing fields, parks and recreation grounds had almost completely disappeared inside the County, and the tide of building was flowing fast and far over the surrounding countryside. The harassed Londoner, in search of solitude, sunshine and healthy recreation, had to travel further and further out.

Within a few months of taking office, the Labour Council had launched its project for a great " Green Belt " around London where the amenities of the existing parks, woodlands and open spaces could be preserved for all time for the healthy enjoyment and recreation of the people. The Council secured the active co-operation of the Local Authorities in the Home Counties, and undertook to contribute £2,000,000 towards the cost of acquiring land for this purpose. Within a very short time many beautiful acres of woods and downlands had been put beyond the reach of the speculative builder. Later, in order to remove any possible doubts that the ownership of these pleasant acres was properly vested in the people of London and the Home Counties, the scheme was embodied in a formal Act of Parliament. Labour had made sure that the " Green Belt " could be worn by London for all time.

Up to the outbreak of war, about 110 square miles, an area almost as large as the whole County of London, had been preserved or provisionally approved for preservation. And even during the war every possible step was taken to prevent the completion of the scheme from being prejudiced when peace returned.

There was also a great deal of work waiting to be done in providing better amenities for open-air rest and recreation within the County boundaries. For many years the County Council Parks had been simply the places where you took the dog for a walk. Forbidding notices stared at you from the grass. The only activity was a few old men silently communing with the sparrows. The dull symmetry of straight asphalt paths and hard

Peace and Progress

benches was walled in by the prim uprightness of the privets.

This was another sphere of Labour's activity in London where one can justly use the phrase about a " startling transformation ". The dog-walks were swiftly transformed into attractive playgrounds for the citizens of London. There were no " Lidos " in London before Labour came to power. At the outbreak of war one of these fine open-air swimming pools with its sun beach was within easy reach of every Londoner. These lidos were intended not only to be places of healthy recreation but also to serve as community centres for the people in the neighbourhood about them. Cafés were built, paddling-pools were provided for the youngsters. The whole family could pass a sunny day in rest and recreation.

Facilities were provided for almost every sort of outdoor recreation—scores of new hard tennis courts, bowling greens, football and cricket pitches were laid down ; dressing-rooms and shower-baths were provided. And the children were not neglected. They had their floodlit gymnasia, their specially equipped playgrounds, their boating-lakes and paddling-pools where they could play, safe from the menace of London streets.

One of the most popular innovations was the holding of free dances in the parks on fine evenings. When the Labour Council introduced this innovation, public approval was so enthusiastic that by the summer of 1939 nine dance bands were engaged for this series of open-air dances. During the summer holidays entertainment was provided for the children and a greatly improved standard of concerts provided for the week-end and evening entertainment of the grown-ups.

The dingy shrubberies disappeared, unnecessary railings were torn down, attractive open-air shelters and more comfortable seats were provided. Flower-beds flourished and spread abundantly. In all, it was a remarkable transformation of what had been the dullest backwaters of London.

There were other reforms which were not so conspicuous to the public gaze, but which were none the less vital for the well-being of the citizens of London. The vigilance of the County Council extends to the vast network of main and storm relief sewers which run below London. Between 1934 and 1939 a great deal was done by the Labour Council to improve and modernise these vital underground ways. The main sewers were enlarged and extensively improved at many points. Over £500,000 was spent in bringing up to date the stations which pumped the outflow from the miles of sewers. For many years, beneath the unsuspecting feet of Londoners, had been the menace that their streets and homes might suddenly be flooded with sewage as the pressure surged up within the sewers during a sudden downpour. The improvements carried out during those years were also of vital importance during the fire-blitz on London, when the enlarged sewers were able to cope swiftly and easily with the deluges of water which were hurled against the flames.

The principles and policies which Labour had advocated in opposition were carried into effect when the power passed into its hands. The bar was removed on the employment of married women as teachers and doctors in the Council's service. The Tory Council had insisted on maintaining this senseless act of sex discrimination, with the result that the Council had been losing many of its most talented professional women, whose value as doctors and teachers was often increased by marriage.

An early act of the Labour Council was to take steps to

Peace and Progress

ensure that all Council contractors were firms who habitually paid and observed fair wages and conditions of employment in respect of their employees. The Council itself, with a staff of over 76,000, was possibly the largest employer in London and the interest and welfare of its own staff were not overlooked. The " emergency cuts " in the pay of firemen and other employees of the Council were restored. New scales of salary and rates of pay were fixed for the supervisory and clerical staffs of the Public Assistance establishment. The engineering staff at all the Council's schools, hospitals and institutions received substantial increases of pay and improved working conditions. Male nurses, domestic staff, manual workers, cooks and cleaners were among the other employees who received better pay and improved conditions of service. Not a single one of these increases could be called extravagant. Labour's vast plans for making London's social and public services the most comprehensive and best run of any city in the world could not be erected on the faulty foundations of ill-paid public servants working under unsatisfactory conditions. The new broom which swept clean many a dark cranny in the Public Assistance and educational services did not neglect its own doorstep.

So the work of improvement and reform went on. Much of it never leaped to meet the public gaze. Very little about it found its way into the headlines. But all of that quiet, unobtrusive work had a direct bearing on the lives, the welfare, the social and economic well-being of the people of London. With sharp vigour, for example, the Council stamped out the practice of certain cinema proprietors of varying the prices of seats in relation to the expected demand. Cinemas in London were compelled to display a plan of their seating arrangements with the prices clearly marked. A provision which did a great

Labour in London

deal to secure a fair deal for the man and his girl in the cinema queue.

Then, too, the quiet efficiency of Alderman Emil Davies as chairman of the Supplies Committee did a great deal to save the public pounds, shillings and pence of Londoners. Under the Labour Council the Supplies Department was expanded to become the central purchasing department for all the various branches of the Council's activities. Compared with 1930, by 1937 the number of requisitions through the Supplies Department had increased from 356,000 to 919,000. Considerable economies were effected by the bulk purchase of many items, and further considerable savings resulted from the standardisation of many of the fittings used in Labour's great housing programme. Baths, boilers, grates, ranges, sinks and doors were only a few of the fitments which by standardisation in design saved the ratepayers many thousands of pounds.

During those years of peace and progress there was hardly an aspect of London's life which was not effected by the march of Labour's progress. An immense building programme which was sweeping away the slums and providing new homes and new opportunities for health and happiness for thousands of Londoners ; new schools and new opportunities for London's children, new hospitals, vastly better equipped hospitals and a whole new range of additional medical services ; community homes for the aged ; better training centres for the physically or economically handicapped ; swimming-pools and sun-beaches, improved allowances for the blind—the previous pages give some idea of how wide and immense was the field covered by the progress of reform. A new and determined social purpose had replaced the inadequate, the shoddy, the parsimonious ways of handling the problems of London's needs and requirements. A new era

Peace and Progress 175

in civic administration had brought swift and far-reaching changes to the metropolis.

The immense plans which called for new homes, new schools, new hospitals and the renovation and reconstruction of hundreds of old and inadequate buildings created a great volume of employment in London. The demand for an enormous range of materials, from nails to intricate medical apparatus, created a stimulating wave of employment in London and much further afield. When Labour came into power it was loudly proclaimed by the Tories that the suggested policies of social improvement would " bankrupt the metropolis ". Today, the policies which Labour advocated in relation to the creation of employment are enshrined in the orthodoxy of a Government White Paper.

What was the cost of this immense programme of construction, renovation and social development ? Before considering the actual details it is interesting to note that when the first part of Labour's programme was already well under way, when Londoners had before them full details of the amount which Labour proposed to spend on new homes, new schools and a vast range of other improvements, the ratepayers of London sent the London Labour Party back to County Hall in 1937 with a greatly increased majority. The ratepayers backed Labour's plans for a better London. Londoners were prepared to pay the piper because they plainly liked the tune.

Furthermore, it should be taken into account that the total expenditure in connection with capital developments in local government does not fall immediately on the rates. Such improvements as schools, houses, hospitals and other items of construction will obviously render service to the community over a period of twenty, fifty, or even seventy years. It is, therefore, only equitable that their cost should be spread over the period of their usefulness. If the expenditure required for Labour's immense housing programme had fallen immediately on the rates the cost would have been prohibitive, but as it was, the immediate cost of this, and many other developments, was secured by borrowing the money and arranging for the repayment of the capital and interest to be spread over periods varying from twenty to eighty years. The cost falling on any one year's rate was accordingly only a fraction of the total expenditure.

The following table shows the extent to which the expenditure of the Labour Council in transforming the municipal services of London was reflected in the County Rates. The rate for the period 1934–5 had already been decided by the Municipal Reformers when Labour came into power, so that the rate for the year ending March 1936 was the first full Labour rate.

LONDON COUNTY COUNCIL RATE

Year ending March	s.	d.
1935	6	$1\frac{1}{2}$
1936	7	0
1937	7	$3\frac{1}{2}$
1938	7	$3\frac{1}{2}$
1939	7	$9\frac{1}{2}$
1940	7	$9\frac{1}{2}$

The increase in rates accordingly amounted by the outbreak of war to 1s. 8d. Twenty pence in each pound of rateable value was the cost of sweeping away acres of slums and building new homes for thousands of Londoners, for re-equipped hospitals and extended medical services which, year by year, paid their rich dividend of lives saved and bodies released from the handicap of disablement and disease, for the schools which provided a new educational endowment for London's children, for the Green Belt, for the Lidos, for a vast

Peace and Progress

range of other improvements and reforms. Londoners had certainly every reason for believing that Labour had given them full value for their money.

There were, however, certain other factors which must be taken into account in adding up this comparatively modest increase. Included in the increase was the cost of restoring the slashing cuts which the Tories had imposed on the unemployed, the schools, and hospital services, and the salaries of teachers, doctors, engineers and many other employees of the Council. Another factor, too, in the increase was the legal decision which relieved the railway companies and the London Passenger Transport Board of a substantial proportion of their assessments. Finally, it should be taken into account that a great deal of the work of slum clearance, renovation and construction should properly have been incurred as the need arose during the long years of apathy and neglect. The accumulated arrears of neglect from the Municipal Reforms administrations was a heavy item in the account. When all these factors are taken into consideration, few will be found to cavil at twenty more pence as the price of a cleaner, healthier, and more efficiently run Capital City than we have ever had before.

It becomes obvious, when we compare the costs with the achievement, that the Labour Council had kept a firm grip on its budget while at the same time ensuring that no essential reform was stinted of the necessary resources. The focal point at which this financial feat was accomplished was in the L.C.C. Finance Committee under the chairmanship of Charles Latham (now Lord Latham). The London County Council has been fortunate in that during the two periods when progressive policies were in full tide in London it was able to secure the services of men of exceptional financial ability to preside over its Finance Committee. When the Progressives ushered in the first period of municipal reform, they appointed as chairman of the Finance Committee Lord Lingen, a former permanent secretary of the Treasury, who kept immoderate schemes of expenditure within proper bounds and whose budgetary methods became the standard for succeeding Councils. So, too, when Labour ushered in the second great period of progress and reform in London, they were fortunate in having as chairman of the Finance Committee a man who had a sure grip of the tangled intricacies of the L.C.C. finance and the money markets, and who knew how to reconcile the needs of the spending department with the requirements of strict budgetary control. The hard and heavy work of the Finance Committee must be regarded as an important factor in the total achievements of Labour in London.

In this field of finance, no less than in the sphere of housing, the achievements of the Labour Council are worthy of record. The vast programme of reform which has been described was carried through without imposing undue burdens on the taxpayers, and a series of large-scale schemes for stock redemption and conversion were carried through which saved hundreds of thousands of pounds of public money. For example, the Finance Committee secured a substantial reduction of the interest payable on some of its stock by redeeming at par in January 1936 the £10,000,000 of $3\frac{1}{2}$ per cent. London County Council Consolidated stock and issuing in its place an equivalent amount of stock at $2\frac{3}{4}$ per cent. This intricate transaction was carried out successfully with an approximate saving in interest during the life of the loan of £68,000 a year. *This loan was seventeen times over-subscribed in five minutes.* For some of the Labour councillors there was a slightly ironical touch about the spectacle of the Banks and great financial houses scram-

Peace and Progress

bling to invest their money in the security of a Labour government at County Hall, when the Tories had loudly proclaimed that Labour in power in the metropolis " would destroy London's credit in the money markets of the world ".

In a reference to this successful transaction the City Editor of *The Times* remarked that " to the extent that the loan will result in fresh spending it will, of course, tend to accentuate the improvement in trade. The prospectus, which is published on our City page, shows that the finances of the L.C.C. are in a flourishing condition."

The finances of the L.C.C. are in a flourishing condition ! It was the epitaph on Tory prophecies. The price of progress had turned out to be prosperity.

Five and a half years was the period of Labour's peacetime work for London. Those who have followed the account will agree that a tremendous amount of work and achievement was crammed into that short space of time. Through the waning years of peace the work of making London a better city to live in had gone on at a swiftly increasing pace. Then the tempo was compelled to falter. The steel required for the immense programme of housing and construction became increasingly difficult to obtain. Skilled man-power was being slowly drained away to the armament factories, to the construction of barracks and airfields. To an increasing extent during those last years of peace, the thoughts and the energies of the Labour Councillors, of the Council's staff and the members of the committees were given over to the preparation for the coming world war.

Then all the plans and the blue prints were pushed aside. The Nazis had begun their march for the conquest of the world. By Government direction building had to cease. The children and their teachers were scattered across the counties of England and Wales. Firemen, Rescue Workers, Ambulance Drivers and Attendants moved into the schools. Labour's work for the people of London had come, so it seemed, temporarily to an end.

But the work of the Labour Council was by no means finished. New and urgent needs arose. New plans had to be made, often in conditions of supreme emergency, for the protection and welfare of the people of London. During the strange and savage period in the capital's history which was about to open, London, more than ever, was to have need for the energy, capacity and courage of her Labour Council.

CHAPTER X

LONDON GOES TO WAR

London appeared to be the most vulnerable city on earth.

The County of London alone covered an area of 117 square miles with a population of more than four million people. Over 2,500 miles of streets. Hundreds of thousands of homes, thousands of warehouses, factories, hospitals, churches and places of entertainment. From the air the main arteries of communication, the trunk roads and railways, looked as thin and as vulnerable as the threads of a spider's web. A few feet below the surface was the no less vital network of lines and channels on which the whole life of that city depended—the lines of heat, light and communication, the channels for gas, water and drains. London would cease to be a habitable city if those lines and channels were permanently broken.

This immense urban area, the vital centre of government and communications, lay a few minutes' flying-time from the coast and was threaded by the Thames, a sure guide to the approaching bomber. No wonder that Goering, when he summoned his bomber squadrons for the assault, described the attack on London as the " blow directed at the heart ".

It did not require the calculating mind of a military strategist to envisage how exposed the millions of people in London were to the perils of air attack, and how grave the consequences of that attack could be to the outcome of any struggle in which Great Britain and her Allies might be engaged. On Air Raid Precautions, as in the other aspects of the defence of Britain, it would be only too easy to pile up yet another formidable indictment against the Conservative Governments which ruled Britain in the years before the war. It was not, in fact, until 1935 that a Special Department of the Home Office was set up to deal with A.R.P. It had a staff of ten housed in seven rooms!

On 10th July 1935 the London County Council received a circular from the Home Office which drew the attention of local authorities to the need for precautionary measures for protecting the civilian population from air attack. The circular went on to stress that the measures suggested were wholly precautionary and the need for then " by no means implied a risk of war in the near future ".

This circular was the limit of effective guidance received by local authorities from the Government for a very long time. For two years, while the Third Reich was spilling across its frontiers, there was complete lack of clear directions about what local authorities should do to protect their citizens and how the cost should be met. The L.C.C., the Metropolitan Borough Councils, and other local authorities pressed this issue on the Government with increasing urgency, seeking adequate powers and clear directions to enable them to protect the civilian population.

It was mainly as the result of the continuous pressure of local authorities that the first Air Raids Precautions Act was passed towards the end of 1937, but it was not until the passing of the London (Allocation of Duties) Order in March 1938 that the tasks and the powers of the L.C.C. were defined.

If the Council had waited passively for these directions the preparations for the protection of London's citizens might have lagged a long way behind. Fortunately the grim lessons of the Spanish cities were more clearly noted in the London Council Chamber than they apparently were in the Cabinet Room across the river. Into all the new plans for the building of homes, schools and hospitals, the Council from 1937 onwards began to incorporate structural precautions against air attack. The whole of the hospital services, the main drainage system and the other essential services were reviewed in the light of their possible functions if London, like Barcelona, should come beneath the bombers' wings. Finally, in December 1937, without waiting further on Government direction, an Air Raids Precautions Sub-Committee was appointed by the Council to co-ordinate and press on with the work of protecting the lives and properties of Londoners against the grim menace which the future was clearly going to bring.

By June 1938, as the result of its own initiative and the more precise allocation of its duties by the Government, the Council had laid the foundations of its own " emergency service ". The Council had become responsible, within the County of London, for the organisation of the Auxiliary Fire Services, the Auxiliary Ambulance Service, the Rescue Service, and for the repair of bridges, sewers, the Thames Embankment, as well as for the provision of shelters for, and the repair of the 100,000 houses and flats owned by the L.C.C. In addition to these emergency services, the Council had the heavy responsibility for ensuring that the main services of the civil government of London, with all its countless points of daily contacts with the lives and interest of Londoners, should be maintained unfalteringly through any emergency.

These heavy burdens were laid on the shoulders of the Labour majority and the Council's staff at a time when the immense schemes for slum clearance and for transforming London's social services were in full progress.

Then came the great rehearsal for war. September 1938 was the first time that our civilian population, like an army, was exercised in the arts of war.

The Munich crisis startled the Government out of its complacency regarding the need for civilian defence. Air Raid Precautions suddenly became a subject of first-class priority.

In this crisis the Government drew extensively upon the resources, organisation and staff of the Council. Sir George Gates, Clerk to the Council, became Chief Air Raids Precaution Officer for the whole of Greater London. Within a few hours the Council's great resources had been thrown into the task of creating a scheme of civilian defence for London.

It was a task which called for desperate improvisations. In that hour of crisis it was discovered by those who were thus hurriedly summoned to the task that, apart from the steps taken by the Council and the other local authorities, no adequate provision for civil defence had been made at all. No system of higher control existed. No system of communications had been designed, no control-room organisation had been laid down, the necessary territorial division of London had not been planned, and no steps had been taken for drawing together and co-ordinating the efforts of the local authorities, the public utility undertakings, and the other numerous and complex organisations by which the life of London was carried on. In the realm of civil defence, London in September 1938 was a city which confronted a catastrophe.

The Chief of the Home Office A.R.P. Department, Mr. C. W. G. Eady, a month later with startling frankness in a civil servant, summarised the position as it was revealed by the Munich crisis. At a meeting held at the Royal United Services Institution on October 26th 1938, he said :

London goes to War

We had no illusions at all about the state of unpreparedness of the country to receive a sudden air attack. We are not prepared. We have hardly begun to prepare. We do not know how all the failures that occurred during the crisis can be avoided next time. . . .

The regulations issued by the A.R.P. Department were probably the sloppiest ever produced by any Government Department. . . .

This has got to be said and it might as well be said at once. People who are known as the governing classes of this country have, broadly speaking, done very little to help local authorities.[1]

The desperately improvised scheme of civilian defence for London was not put to the test. The Munich crisis passed. It was " peace in our time ", and London had one more year to put its system of civil defence on a better basis.

The year which followed was one of intense activity for the Labour Council. The concentrated attention which the Council gave to the civilian defence of the capital is shown by the creation of a full Air Raids Precautions Committee in December 1938, and in the special measures adopted for enrolling volunteers in the Ambulance and Fire Services, in the adoption of the hospitals to the estimated needs of wartime, in the provision of a simplified system of tender in order to speed up the provision of shelters and in the suspension of non-essential public work so that all available labour could be diverted to A.R.P. work.

During the same period a more effective A.R.P. organisation was being evolved. Under the Regional Commissioners Act, 1939, the country was divided into regions, for each of which one or more Regional Commissioners were appointed who were directly responsible to the Home Secretary. No. 5 (London) Region was

[1] *Daily Telegraph*, October 27, 1938.

approximately co-terminous with the Metropolitan Police District. The Regional Commissioners were charged with the responsibility of stimulating and guiding the preparation by local authorities of air raid precaution schemes, securing that these schemes conformed in general with the principles laid down by the Government and for exercising an overriding financial control of the expenditure incurred by the local authorities.

During the same year the Civil Defence Act, 1939, was passed. This Act was mainly concerned with provision of air-raid shelters both for the public and for employees at commercial and industrial undertakings. By midsummer of 1939 the main structure of Civil Defence had taken its wartime shape.

The following table shows the allocation of responsibility for the various air-raid services and between the London County Council and the Metropolitan Borough Councils.

Pre-Raid Services.
Evacuation Service (L.C.C.).
Public and domestic shelter provision (M.B.C. except at L.C.C. tenement dwellings).

Raid Services.
Fire Guard Service (M.B.C.).
Wardens' Service (M.B.C.).
Report and Control Centre Service (M.B.C.).
Auxiliary Fire Service (L.C.C. up to 17. 8. 41—National Fire Service thereafter).
Light Rescue Service (M.B.C., formerly the Stretcher Party Service).
Heavy Rescue Service (L.C.C.).
Auxiliary Ambulance Service (L.C.C.).
First Aid Posts Service (M.B.C.).
Decontamination Service (M.B.C.).
Hospital Casualty Service (Ministry of Health, utilising in the main L.C.C. hospitals).

Post Raid Services.
Information Service (M.B.C.).
Rest Centre Service (L.C.C.).

Meals Service (L.C.C.).
Rehousing and Billeting Organisation (M.B.C.).
Debris Disposal Service (L.C.C.).

Repair Services.
Roads (M.B.C.).
Bridges (L.C.C.).
Sewers (L.C.C.).
Thames Embankment (L.C.C.).
Housing (M.B.C., except at L.C.C. Housing Estates).
Electricity (Supply company concerned).
Gas (Supply company concerned).
Public Transport (London Passenger Transport Board or Railway company concerned).

The co-ordination of these services was the responsibility of the Regional Commissioners. For this purpose the London Region was, until November 1943, divided into nine groups, five of which covered the administrative County of London. After November 1943 the number of groups in London was reduced to four. The function of the Groups was almost exclusively operational, an important feature being that of securing mutual aid between local civil defence authorities in the Group, or should the Group resources be exhausted of obtaining, through Regional Headquarters, additional assistance from a neighbouring Group which might not be so hard-pressed. There was thus created for London a three-tier operational system in civil defence built up in the Borough as its basic unit, in which the system of control ran from the Borough Control Centre to the Group Centre and from there passing on to the Regional Headquarters. It was a system designed to secure the maximum fluidity in man-power and equipment to cope equally with concentrated as well as scattered raids.

There were still gaps to be filled in this system when war came on 3rd September 1939. Two days previously a state of emergency had been declared and the whole A.R.P. organisation, as well as other Government measures, were brought into operation. The Emergency Powers (Defence) Act put an immense concentration of power into the hands of the Central Government and a parallel concentration of power was taking place in the realm of Local Government. All over Britain the powers and duties vested in the elected Councils and their committees were concentrated in the hands of small Emergency Committees. In some parts of the country, the creation of these Emergency Committees, vested with exceptional powers, was welcomed by reactionary ruling cliques as an opportunity to grasp untrammelled control, free from the inconvenience of public scrutiny and from the democratic checks of open Council discussion. But the Emergency Committee of the London County Council desired no such extension of power. Within a few months the meetings of the Council were resumed on a monthly basis and the main committee system was largely brought back into operation.

In the meantime, in those first days of emergency, the responsibilities were crowding in upon the Council. When the Armed forces were mobilised they moved into barracks and camps prepared to receive them. With the men and women of Civil Defence the position was not so easy. Their action stations had to be requisitioned and made ready at the last minute—halls, garages and schools, many of them still containing their peacetime equipment. It called for an immense effort of organisation to provide literally overnight, beds, food and equipment for this great civilian army.

There were very few hitches in bringing the detailed plans into operation. The halls and schools were taken over, the control rooms were occupied. The Wardens' posts, often in dark cellars and many strange subterranean crevices of London, received the men and women who were to occupy them for the long vigil of Civil Defence.

London goes to War

The ambulances and fire-engines moved to their war stations. London swiftly became familiar with the black uniforms of the civilian army which had been summoned up to defend our cities in the era of the new and terrible ways of war. Without any pause an intensive system of training and rehearsal was brought into operation.

At the same time, a great and equally orderly movement of London's population was taking place. During the first week in September about a third of London's population was on the move. Men and women were moving out of London to their places in the armed forces, key workers were moving off to their appointed war jobs. Civil servants were moving to their "emergency quarters". There was, too, a concentric movement of families drawing closer together, daughters divided from their husbands by the call-up moving back to their old homes, a general instinctive tightening of families before the incalculable menace of war. In addition there was a certain amount of voluntary evacuation. But having regard to the vivid knowledge which Londoners had of the fate of the citizens of Shanghai, Guernica and Barcelona, the numbers who moved out of London for reasons of personal security were very small indeed. Right from the beginning the majority of Londoners were staying put and standing firm.

The London County Council itself was responsible for a large share of the controlled exodus from London.

The Council had been charged with organising the evacuation of all schoolchildren in the Greater London Area, together with the mothers of children under 5, blind persons, and mentally and physically defective children. Altogether a possible total of 1,300,000 persons were covered by this immense evacuation scheme.

Even those who were responsible for drawing up the plans were amazed at the smoothness with which the

Labour in London

wide range of operations were carried out when the time came.

The Council's evacuation plan reached into thousands of homes in the London area. It meant a great rending of family ties, the uprooting of the children, mothers with young children leaving their husbands behind to fend for themselves. Mothers, husbands and children accepted the sad necessity of parting, calmly and sanely. The mothers who saw their children off smiled as they waved to the young faces at the window. It was the self-imposed discipline of the people, children and adults, which made it possible to operate the vast Evacuation Plan as smoothly as a well-rehearsed manoeuvre. The buses moved from the assembly points to the stations. The long crowded trains drew out, running to a schedule which had long ago been arranged.

The Council was responsible for moving the children and their teachers, the Local Authorities in the receiving areas becoming responsible for their billeting and welfare at the other end. Some 20,000 of London's teachers went with the children to carry on with their care and education in the reception areas. There was, however, one group of children which the Council kept under its own supervision—the children who were handicapped by some physical or mental defect. These were the children who were cared for in the Council's Special Schools and Hospitals, or who were brought to school each day in special children's ambulances. In war, the Council's special help and supervision for these children was continued.

Camps, houses and hostels in the reception areas were taken over and administered by the Council for them. During that first anxious week the ambulances were carrying away from London those children who could have done so little to help themselves among all the possible emergencies of war. For many of them it was their first experience of the countryside. The war, with its strange twists of fate, had brought the chance of green fields, fresh air, sunshine and treatment and training for those who most needed it. By this chance of war, opportunities for health and happiness were to open out for many children during the months and years ahead.

This movement of 500,000 children, with 20,000 teachers, was the largest of the evacuation schemes carried out by the L.C.C. But there were smaller schemes which went no less smoothly.

Over 16,000 beds in the L.C.C. hospitals had been allocated to the Emergency Hospitals Organisation. On the outbreak of war, a large number of patients were moved out of these " front-line hospitals " to more secure quarters in the country. Some of the twenty-two ambulance trains staffed and equipped by the Council for the Ministry of Health were used for this evacuation.

During the same week the evacuation of the blind, the aged people and the adult mental defectives in the special hospitals was carried out by the Council. By the end of that week the Council had been responsible for the evacuation of nearly three-quarters of a million people.

During that time many of the other emergency plans laid by the Council were brought into operation. The hospitals were stocked with special equipment and medical supplies, shelters were completed on the Council estates, special measures were taken to protect the main drainage system and to supply millions of gallons of water to the fire-fighting services, certain of the Council's services were decentralised, the work of the new Waterloo Bridge and Wandsworth Bridge was speeded up—in short, a hundred schemes for the protection of Londoners and their interests were brought into operation.

Then the concentration of effort was spent. The plans with all their minute details had been brought into operation. Every precaution that could be taken at the time had been taken. And the skies above London were conspicuously empty of enemy planes.

It was the period of the " phoney war ". But those who were responsible for London's Civil Defence didn't share in any sense of anticlimax. The organisation of Civil Defence had been drafted, but thousands of men and women had to be trained in the use of equipment, in the tactics of fire-fighting and rescue, had to acquire the knowledge and skill which was going to serve them and London so well.

It is perhaps worth recalling that during this phase of the war a light-headed section of the Press was indulging in a vigorous campaign about the " extravagant expenditure lavished on Air Raid Precautions ". These papers talked lightly of the " idle armies of civil defence workers ". " Idle " was a slightly ironical word to apply to the intensive training that these workers were undertaking at that time. It would be still more difficult to find appropriate words to describe the conduct of the section of the Press which was responsible for this campaign.

The Council resisted all attempts to cut down or in any way to reduce the effectiveness of their precautions.

How large were the civil defence forces which were equipped and organised by the L.C.C.

At the outbreak of war the largest force mobilised by the L.C.C. was the Auxiliary Fire Service. The peacetime London Fire Brigade of 2,000 officers and men, housed in sixty fire-stations, was expanded into the London Fire Service with a strength of 25,000 men and women stationed at 400 premises. Their equipment included 2,800 pumps of varying gallon-per-minute capacity, 2,400 towing units, 500 cars, 860 motor cycles, together

London goes to War

with certain special apparatus, and 40 river-boats and barges for fighting riverside fires and relaying water.

Experience during periods of heavy raids, particularly in provincial districts, showed that a greater degree of central control was desirable to secure the rapid mobilisation of all resources in the district where the need was greatest and to overcome the undefined relative status of the chief officers of the various brigades when unified command had to be taken at a large fire. It fell to Herbert Morrison, as Minister of Home Security, to achieve the only degree of " Nationalisation " achieved during the war. On 17th August 1941 all fire-fighting services, including the peacetime brigades, were transferred to the direct control of the Home Office as one unified National Fire Service, and the London County Council was relieved of the responsibility for maintaining one of the largest of its civil defence services.

There was still, however, much work to be performed by the Council on behalf of the National Fire Service. For example, the bombing of London had made available large sites on which static reservoirs could be erected, and the Council swiftly erected storage space for 200,000,000 gallons of water.

The peacetime ambulance service, operated by the Council, comprised about 400 offices and men and a fleet of 180 vehicles based at 6 general stations and 14 accident stations. This service was expanded to nearly 9,000 men and women distributed over 120 stations with a fleet of 1,600 vehicles. Experience under actual raid conditions led to considerable reductions in the strength of this service.

The Rescue Service had no peacetime counterpart. At first the duty of organising this service rested with the Metropolitan Borough Councils, but early in 1939 it was transferred to the Council. At the outbreak of war the service was rapidly developed into one of 10,000 men, mostly recruited from the building industry. Each squad consisted of ten men, equipped with lorry and tackle for rescue and shoring. In addition to these squads, mobile squads with heavy cranes and skilled engineers were formed to assist with rescue work where large buildings were involved.

The work of the Heavy Rescue Service was supplemented later on by the Light Rescue Service formed from the Stretcher Party Service, of about 4,000 strong, trained and equipped for rescuing casualties from the less serious incidents. This service, like the Stretcher Party Service it replaced, was provided by the Metropolitan Borough Councils.

The Debris Disposal Service was transferred to the Council when it became evident that the resources of the Borough Councils were not adequate for the job. The main tasks of the service were the clearance of debris from the roads in order to maintain communications, to give assistance quickly to people anxious to rescue the contents of their wrecked homes and to clear away the destroyed buildings.

While the Debris Disposal Service was developing it was assisted by thousands of troops of the Royal Engineers and Pioneer Corps. At one period the civilian strength rose to 23,700, which enabled it to give assistance to the Rescue Service in the urgent work of removing debris at incidents to enable trapped people to be rescued.

During the course of the war the Council was called upon to organise several new emergency services for London. But these were the main civil defence services which were maintained by the L.C.C.

The men and women of these services formed a substantial part of the armies of Civil Defence, which were soon to be flung into the Battle of London.

CHAPTER XI

REST CENTRES AND EMERGENCY FEEDING

THE first bombs fell in the County of London on the night of 24th August, wrecking small houses in Shoreditch and Bethnal Green, and causing fires in the City and Poplar.

This was the prelude to the main attack which began on 7th September and was renewed night after night without respite for eight long weeks, until 2nd November, when there was a brief lull; but the attacks were soon renewed and continued until well into the summer of 1941.

We cannot pursue the narrative of those grim and agonising weeks in London's history. The story of the Civil Defence Services has been told in some details in the fine official account, *Front Line*, and already there are hundreds of more personal accounts by those who experienced that fantastic deluge of bombs and by those who fought the flames.

Lord Latham, who had taken over the leadership of the Council when Herbert Morrison joined the Government as Minister of Supply, and had assumed the Chairmanship of the Civil Defence and General Purposes Committee, described the feelings of all at County Hall when, speaking of those times, he said, " the courage and fortitude of Londoners, the heroism and endurance of our Civil Defence Forces have given a new depth of meaning to our determination to build a London which is really worthy of our people ".

The casualties in the Battle of London mercifully did not come up to official expectations. The beds in the hospitals were never filled to capacity, and on only one occasion were the full resources of the Auxiliary Ambulance Service called into action—on 16th April 1941, when 2,476 casualties were taken to hospitals and first-aid posts by ambulance vehicles.

There was, however, another class of casualty whose number far exceeded the Government's estimates. They were the people whose homes were destroyed and those, still more numerous, who had to leave their homes while delayed action bombs were dealt with. It was the duty of the Rest Centre Service to provide food, shelter and other comforts to these shaken and homelsss folk.

The Ministry of Health was responsible for the provision of the Rest Centre Service. The Ministry specified the number of Rest Centres required and the stocks of food and equipment to be provided for this Service. The Council itself was called upon to obtain and equip the premises and to staff and maintain the Service.

Some 150 " first line " Rest Centres were established, staffed by the L.C.C. Social Welfare Department, each Centre providing protected sleeping accommodation for upwards of 200 people. In addition there were 50 second- and third-line centres which were brought into operation when the need arose, with the assistance of the Women's Voluntary Service.

The first centres were brought into operation in the early hours of Sunday, 25th August, but it was not until the full-scale attack on 7th September that the great tide of shaken and homeless people began to pour into the Rest Centres. On Sunday, 8th September, there were 10,000 people in the Centres and 48 hours later the numbers were approaching 16,000.

These homeless folk might not need hospital treatment, but they were in urgent need of care, rest and food. Thousands of them, during these grim winter months, came out of their shelters into a dawn reeking with smoke and dust to find their homes had been stricken into fantastic puddings of bricks and broken furniture. Others were pulled out of their homes, uninjured but acutely feeling the experience. Into these shattered homes had gone all the work and care of a lifetime ; under those piles of debris were all those souvenirs which are so infinitely precious to us all—the photos of the youngsters, the wedding presents, the piano which had been purchased with so much sacrifice.

All the resources of the L.C.C. were put behind the task of providing food, equipment and nursing attention for the Rest Centres. The Social Welfare Staff carried on a 24-hour service at Centres, assisted by volunteers, nursing staff and teachers. Incredible difficulties were overcome. For instance, a Council Central kitchen supplying a large number of meals to 14 Centres was put out of action. A firm of caterers which agreed to supply these meals received a direct hit during the night, yet by the following day excellent meals were being provided by some of the Council's Institutes.

When the water mains were hit at one Centre, the Social Welfare officers went out through the raid to cart water, so that the sanitation might be kept going and those in the Centres could have a wash before going to work in the morning.

The Nazis poured their hail of bombs on London. They blasted thousands of homes out of existence ; they killed 12,696 and wounded 20,000 citizens of London during the most intense three months of the Blitz. But the Nazis never found the weak spot they were looking for. And it was there, in the smoke and grime of embattled London, that the tide of war began to turn. The courage and determination of our people—the people in the Rest Centres, the people whose homes were shattered and their more fortunate neighbours who " missed it "—had won one of the most decisive battles in the history of mankind.

Labour in London

During the whole period of the European phase of the World War—from 3rd September 1939 to 8th May 1945—a total of 259,438 homeless people found refuge in the L.C.C. Rest Centres. Of this total, 162,051 were admitted during the heavy raiding of 1940 and 1941; 20,709 during the isolated raids of 1942, 1943 and 1944; and 76,678 during the period of the V1 and V2 attacks from the 13th June 1944 to the end of the war.

The largest number of people accommodated in the Centres at any one time was 18,615 in 145 centres on the night of 16th October 1940. The highest number of admissions during one period of 24 hours was 14,658 following the night raid of 16th April 1941.

During the flying bomb and rocket attacks the total population of the centres reached 10,000 on one occasion only—on 3rd July 1944, when 10,025 people were accommodated in 104 Centres. The highest number of admissions was 4,441 on 18th June 1944.

Although available at all times for their primary function of caring for the homeless, the Rest Centres found a variety of ways in which to be of service to the people of London during the war.

As agents for the Londoners' Meals Service, they undertook the provision of dinners, teas and breakfasts for school children, and at one time were cooking and serving 35,000 meals a day in the Centres for the children.

To enable mothers of young children to undertake war work the Rest Centre Service established day nurseries in 29 of the Centres in which over 500 toddlers aged 2 to 5 years were cared for.

When the programme for first-aid repairs to London's bombed houses called for the help of thousands of building trade operatives from the provinces, the Rest Centre Service offered 62 of its Centres for use as temporary

Rest Centres and Emergency Feeding 199

hostels, and from October 1944 to the end of the war 5,643 of the men were accommodated in these centres.

On many occasions during the war the Service was able to be of help to the Ministry of Health and the Foreign Office by providing, at a moment's notice, meals and overnight accommodation for parties of British repatriates and French, Belgian and Dutch refugees from the Continent who were brought to London and had no homes to which they could immediately go. On the outbreak of the war with Japan a party of over 100 consular and other officials and their families from the Far East were accommodated for several days in a London Rest Centre while arrangements were made to find homes for them in this country.

Twelve of the Rest Centres have been used, at the request of the Canadian Government, for the overnight accommodation of some 3,200 British wives of Canadian servicemen and their children who passed through London on their way to their new homes in Canada.

As a part of the Rest Centre Service, the Council, at the request of the Ministry of Health, established 12 Rest Homes for infirm and aged people who had been bombed out of their homes and who were too feeble to be set up again in homes of their own. Some 500 old folk are now cared for in these Homes in comfortable and homelike surroundings. They are free to go and come as they choose, and keep their independence by paying for their maintenance so far as their means allow.

During the flying-bomb attacks several of the Homes were severely damaged and many more old people were admitted to the Rest Centres as the result of damage to their homes. Under the conditions then obtaining it was impracticable to establish additional Rest Homes and the Service therefore organised the evacuation of some 550 old people to provincial homes and hostels.

At the request of the Ministry of Health it also made all the necessary arrangements for over 600 old people who had been bombed out in the neighbouring counties of Essex, Kent and Surrey to be sent in evacuation parties to safer areas.

All who came in contact with the Rest Centre Service paid tribute to its efficiency and to the manner in which it adapted itself to the requirements of the people who were experiencing the aerial bombardment. But to the people who came to the Rest Centres, their clothes powdered with the dust from their shattered homes, themselves shaken by the experience, the thing which mattered most was the homely and comforting atmosphere which had been created at the Centres. Trained nurses and welfare workers knew the right things to provide and do to restore calm and confidence. There was always room for precious belongings salvaged from the debris; there were kennels for the household cats and dogs which had often to be stubbornly rescued before their owners sought refuge. Provision could be made for the old lady's canary, and a temporary home was even found for a young and vociferous donkey which came trotting into the Centre, as eager as its owner to tell the Rest Centre staff about its experience.

The homeless were gathered into the Rest Centres, the injured were swiftly removed to the care of the Hospitals Emergency Service. But for those who remained behind the Blitz had brought a host of new problems. There was plaster to be shovelled out of the rooms, roofs to be mended, gaping windows which had somehow to be sealed. And, above all, there was the problem of food.

There were thousands of Londoners with food in their larders who could not cook it. Thousands of women found themselves deprived of even the warm comfort of the kitchen teapot. The water was gone. The gas and

Rest Centres and Emergency Feeding 201

electricity were off. The mains and cables had been shattered by the bombardment.

It was out of this emergency that the now familiar Londoners' Meal Service has grown. Field kitchens which could be fuelled with coal and debris timber were swiftly set up on cleared sites, school playgrounds and other open spaces. " Emergency cooks "—the ever resourceful London teachers, volunteer housewives and skilled hotel chefs—served up thousands of meals on the primitive but effective field kitchens. To these points came people with their own utensils to purchase food and take it home to eat.

Within a few days the service of meals was brought indoors. Schools, church-halls and other premises were taken over. By Christmas 1940, 130 Londoners' Meal Service centres were in operation. The repair of broken roads and fractured mains and cables went swiftly forward. But the meal centres survived the passing of the emergency. Another need of wartime life had made itself apparent—well-cooked, substantial meals for the people who were pouring in increasing numbers into the war work which was steadily expanding despite the remorseless bombardment by the Luftwaffe. The Minister of Food therefore asked the Council to develop a permanent wartime service of meals for Londoners.

Thus, out of London's emergency and the L.C.C. swift response to the needs of the people, was born the idea of the British Restaurant, which has served the needs of war-workers in nearly every part of the British Isles.

London alone did not adopt the new name of British Restaurant. The title " Londoners' Meal Service " was retained with affection and pride for the chain of over two hundred restaurants which served 340,000 meals to Londoners every week.

The V-weapon attack brought a new phase in the

development of the Londoners' Meal Service. The first V1 bomb fell in Grove Road, Bow, in June 1944, and disclosed the pattern of damage and destruction to which this weapon was to subject London. From the first day of the attack it became clear that the Londoners' Meal Service must bring food to the people at the " incident ". The people would not move away from their blasted and shattered homes. Many would not leave the scene even for a few minutes to go to a restaurant. Some were anxious about relatives and friends ; some were waiting for the men who would come to do first-aid repairs ; some were waiting for vans to remove their belongings to a new home ; many were reluctant to leave their houses when the doors had been blown out, and the vast majority were too busy " clearing up the mess " to pause and struggle with broken stoves and dirtied saucepans in the effort to secure a meal.

The Londoners' Meal Service, therefore, sent hot meals in containers made on the thermos principle and the meals were served at the kerbside as the vehicles proceeded along the streets in the neighbourhood of the " incident ".

Between 13th June 1944 and 27th March 1945 the service operated in the streets on 240 occasions during the 288 days of the attacks.

This " kerbside feeding " played an important part in sustaining the high morale of the Londoner at a critical period of the war.

Chapter XII

EDUCATION IN WARTIME

The story of wartime education in London is an account of interrupted beginnings. The attempt to provide a system of education amid the perils and distractions of wartime London became a heartbreaking task for all connected with the Education Services.

The impact of the war on the education services in London was immediate and shattering. All the work of the schools came to an end. The majority of the children of London were scattered across the counties of England.

It was the Government's intention that all the schools in London should be closed for the duration of the war. The schools were accordingly regarded as no longer required for their original purposes and they were placed at the disposal of Civil Defence and the other Government services. The central staff of the Education Department were allocated to other duties and the teachers who did not accompany the children to the reception areas were loaned to other services.

It was immediately clear, however, that by no means all the school children had left London with the official evacuation teams. But there were no schools and no system of education to provide for their needs. The problem became more acute when, within a few weeks, the steady drift back of the children from the country began. London was in danger of taking a step backwards to the period when children roamed the streets in undisciplined bands, and a new illiteracy threatened to darken the minds of another generation of London's children.

Confronted with the danger, it was the teachers who remained in London who took the first steps to cope with the situation. These devoted men and women, on their own initiative, began to seek out the children in order to bring them again under some sort of educational influence. In private homes, in clubs, and in empty rooms, they began getting the children in tiny groups to work. All ages and both sexes were to be found together in those strange wartime classes. There were few textbooks, no blackboards except those improvised with boards and paint, and none of the standard educational equipment which had been so abundantly available in the re-organised Council schools.

The initial impulse came from the teachers, but the Council swiftly caught up the work which they had begun. Some of the school buildings were re-claimed from the services which had occupied them, educational equipment was made available and the teaching staff were recalled from the services to which they had been loaned. The classes which included children of all ages were re-organised to allow normal educational progress to be resumed. By December 1939 the fabric of the London educational system had been partly restored.

It was necessary to add to the number of schools to keep pace with the homeward drift of children to London. The shelter accommodation at the schools had to be swiftly expanded, but there always remained the persistent anxiety of having such an increasing number of children in London, instead of their being scattered over the comparative safety of the reception areas.

Then the Blitz shattered all that which had been so laboriously achieved. The swift tide of evacuation carried the majority of the children away. The number of school children in London during the Blitz sank to about 81,000, of whom some 23,000 were sent to school. A number of teachers were called in to help with the new emergency services such as the Rest Centres and the

Education in Wartime

Londoners' Meals Service. Many school buildings were demolished or rendered unusable. Finally, once again, the Government ordered the closing of all schools in the London area.

After an interval, among all the strange abnormalities of life in the blitzed and blacked-out capital, the Council resumed responsibility for the education of the children who were acquiring such vivid lessons in international morality. The schools were reopened and the whole complex business of ascertaining the need, getting the children together, securing the staff and finding the accommodation had to be done all over again.

With the ending of the Blitz, the tide of evacuees once again turned for home. By May 1943 over 230,000 children in London were accommodated in over 700 schools, staffed by 8,250 teachers.

In November 1942 the Government had suspended organised evacuation from London, and in the periods of the lulls in the air attack, the school population of London settled near the quarter-million mark. In the emergency schools, as far as circumstances would permit, educational progress was resumed. But at the best it was a halting sort of progress, interrupted by the effects of spasmodic raids, in bricked-up and blacked-out class-rooms, with the children's minds continually distracted by the excitements and dangers of wartime London.

The attack by the V-weapons lead to another swift disruption of education in London. Organised evacuation was resumed and the special branch of County Hall worked day and night while the flood of evacuees once again poured out of London. During the 37 days on which parties of evacuees left the metropolis, 435 special trains were run from the London termini. The heaviest load was 35,107 on 11th July 1944, and the lightest was

257 on 8th September, the day on which the last official evacuation train left London.

The total number of people who registered to go with the official parties was 331,223, of whom 276,501 presented themselves for evacuation. They comprised 58,664 mothers, including expectant mothers, 59,793 children under five, 57,395 children over 5, and 100,649 unaccompanied children of school age.

So much for the interruptions and handicaps of wartime education in London. It is still difficult to assess the full effects in the outlook and mental development of the children who experienced it. We have, however, very definite evidence that their physical development was unimpaired. The medical officers in charge of the school medical services have put it on record that the health of London schoolchildren showed no signs of deterioration during the long years of war.

The school medical services were fully maintained in order to watch over the health and physical development of the schoolchildren. The introduction of food rationing with the anxiety that the children should suffer as little as possible from the effects of food shortage gave a new importance to school feeding. The existing school feeding arrangements were rapidly extended and school canteens were opened to provide meals for the growing number of children whose mothers were going out to work. The Londoners' Meal Service took over the development of the schoolchildren's meals service. A nutritious meal, with plenty of variety in the choice of dishes, was made available to London children at a maximum charge of 4*d.*, or 6*d.* in the case of full-time students under 19. The number of children provided with a midday meal was 2,000 at the end of 1940. From then on the service expanded rapidly to meet the growing demand. The number had grown to 10,000 a day by

Education in Wartime

October 1941, to 44,000 a day in October 1942, and by June 1944 over 85,000, or more than one-third of the children, were having a midday meal at school.

With the increasing employment of women in the war industries the Education Committee extended the day nursery accommodation for children under school age. Provision had also to be made for children whose mothers' work time extended beyond the school hours. Over a hundred Play Centres were opened in various parts of London where the children could stay and play until they were able to go home. At many of these Play Centres, tea and breakfast were provided. Furthermore, in the school holidays, Holiday Clubs were set up where the children could go who would otherwise be left to their own devices while the parents were at work. Teachers, doctors and nurses kept an unobtrusive but effective watch on the health and well-being of the children at these centres. It is one of the strange anomalies of war that the wartime generation of London's children were to prove possibly healthier and better developed than any of their predecessors. In that result, the wartime medical services and feeding arrangements of the L.C.C. played an important part.

The majority of the schoolchildren of London remained in the reception areas, and the direct responsibility for their education passed to the local authorities there. Although those children had passed out of the direct control of the L.C.C. they had not passed beyond the interest of their London Council. The L.C.C.'s concern for their welfare went a long way beyond the requirements of the official Evacuation Scheme—particularly in the case of children who had to go to areas where the educational facilities were not so good as those provided by the L.C.C. services. In addition to the teachers, L.C.C. officials moved into many of the reception areas to assist the local authorities. Thousands of tons of educational equipment, desks, drawing-pins, cinematographs and radio equipment—were sent to the reception areas. In every possible way the L.C.C. remained watchful of the educational interests and welfare of the children who had been exiled from London. When, for example, the shortage of agricultural labour necessitated the Government calling for children to volunteer, the Education Committee, in order to safeguard the welfare of London children, sent a letter to all education authorities in the reception areas to inform them on their views on the subject.

Nor were the needs of continued and adult education in London neglected. The evening and technical institutes could not open during the first months of the war because there was at that time a general tendency for people to remain at home after nightfall and because the buildings themselves required a great deal of material and labour to black them out. There was, however, a swift regeneration of Londoners' interest in continued education. Classes were organised at week-ends as a temporary measure, and as the material and labour became available, the institutes were blacked out and once again Londoners went in tens of thousands to their evening classes. The Blitz scattered the majority of the students, but a number of the classes " went underground ". The L.C.C. followed the Londoners' unquenchable demand for learning by organising classes in many of the large air-raid shelters in London during the Blitz.

The lecturers who took these classes will always have a vivid recollection of these strange nights in the London shelters. The intent faces of the students, youthful, middle-aged and old. The children who played and tumbled over the bundles of blankets. The sudden flickering of the lights and the deep concussion of the

Education in Wartime

bomb-falls. The vast roar of the barrage. And in the midst of the destruction and the uproar that calm, unquenchable thirst for knowledge, like a conscious and collective assertion of the faculty of human reason against the forces of unreason which were seeking to dominate the world.

That grim wartime interlude in London education is over. In May 1945 the evacuation trains began to run in reverse.

The L.C.C. had formulated many of their plans for the time when the last siren would have sounded over London and the children would have come home. New schools had been planned, and still wider educational opportunities had been envisaged for the children of the metropolis.

And within a few months of the children's return a new vista of educational progress was opened up by the return of the Labour Government to power.

Chapter XIII

SOCIAL WELFARE IN WARTIME

It was a fairly radical process of change which had altered the old Public Assistance Department into the new Social Welfare Service of the Council. But the war worked an even swifter transformation in the scope of the service and in the range of duties undertaken by its staff.

At the outbreak of war there were some 70,000 people on outdoor relief, and about 9,000 were maintained in eighteen residential institutions. As the war continued there was a steep decline in the number of applicants for both outdoor and institutional relief. In August 1940, on the passing of the Old Age and Widows' Pension Act, about 32,000 persons who had previously had their pensions supplemented by outdoor relief were transferred to the Public Assistance Board. By the fourth year of war the number on outdoor relief had fallen to 12,000, of whom only a mere handful were able-bodied " employables ", while the number of those who were in institutions had fallen from 9,000 to 5,400. A very large number of aged veterans, many of whom had little, if any, regular employment since the last war, had joined the ranks of the war workers for another phase of employment in the Second World War.

The organisation of the service was adapted to the circumstances of war. From the outbreak of hostilities, the payment of relief was made in a large percentage of cases in their own homes, and the hours of attendance at the Welfare Stations were " staggered " to avoid the gathering of any number of people at the stations. Except during the crucial period of the Battle of London, between

Social Welfare in Wartime

October 1940 and February 1941, the Area Committees continued to function throughout the war, meeting monthly or fortnightly, and carrying out with the adjudication officers the work of the district sub-committees as well.

The Council exercised continual vigilance to ensure that the changes in economic conditions and social habits did not affect the standards of relief. The scales of relief were increased on four occasions, and particular attention was given to the difficulties created by clothes rationing, with the consequent disappearance of the street markets and other second-hand sources of supply.

The welfare stations and institutions suffered very heavily during the 1940-1 blitz. Many of the welfare stations and every one of the institutions were damaged. Fortunately the casualties were not heavy, although all of the major weapons of the Luftwaffe, from canisters of incendiaries to land-mines, at one time or another, scored hits on the Council's institutions.

There were many occasions when immediate evacuation of an institution had to take place while the raid was still in progress. These emergency evacuations all occurred at night, and in one instance over 400 aged men and women were hurriedly evacuated while the bombs were still falling. The shaken old folk with their hurriedly snatched bundles were moved by the London Passenger Transport Board buses summoned by an urgent call to the London Civil Defence Region Transport Pool.

Even in the midst of these hurried evacuations, the Welfare Officers in charge tried to ensure that old friends were kept together, and as large parties as possible were sent to the same destination. Some of these old folk were especially harried by the malice of the enemy, and were bombed out on two or three occasions. The old people displayed a surprising degree of cheerfulness and mental resiliency in the midst of these grim experiences, although some of the old ladies suddenly displayed a power of expression which astonished even the case-hardened officers of the Welfare Department.

During more settled periods, the effort was continued to maintain as high as possible the standard of life inside the institutions and to improve the amenities. The Council's film projectors were in constant use, and the local youth committees associated with the evening institutes filled the gaps caused by the disappearance of the professional concert parties. The vast majority of the inmates by the beginning of 1943 were aged people, and a step was taken which greatly added to their contentment when it was decided that, under the powers given by the Poor Law Amendment Act, 1938, each inmate over 65 should be given a weekly personal allowance in cash, in addition to the usual allowance of sweets or tobacco.

The steep fall in the number of those who required relief brought no relaxation to the staff of the Social Welfare Department. While one set of duties diminished, others swiftly expanded. The Social Welfare Department acted as the agent for the Government in equipping and staffing the Rest Centres. It was the devotion, courage and initiative of the Social Welfare staff at the Rest Centres which coped with the many unpredictable difficulties during the first period of the continuous day and night attacks on London. There were many occasions when the resourcefulness of the staff was tested to the utmost limit. Good food and plentiful hot drinks were the care of the Rest Centre service. People with a good meal inside them could stand up to things which would provoke panic or angry disorder from hungry and uncared for people. At all costs, the meals service of the Centres had to be kept going. But with broken mains, the

Social Welfare in Wartime

swift provision of a hot meal became a task of exceptional difficulty.

Other duties crowded in upon the Welfare Committee. The Government relied on the experience of the Social Welfare Service in dealing with the distressed and destitute folk of London to cope with the immediate needs of the people of Europe who fled before the tide of war to seek refuge in these lands.

When in the spring of 1940 the swift overpowering thrust of the German Panzers began to sweep across France and the Low Countries, the Government asked the Council as a matter of foremost urgency to prepare for the reception of foreign refugees. The Government informed the Council that the first parties could be expected to arrive within a few days and that reception centres should be prepared to receive up to 10,000 refugees at one time. It was the intention that, after a brief rest and medical and security examinations, refugees should be passed on to the Metropolitan Borough Councils for billeting with English families, or for placing in furnished apartments or empty houses.

Once again the Social Welfare staff had to improvise at urgent speed. Nearly all suitable accommodation had been commandeered for war purposes and it became a strenuous task to find suitable quarters for the expected flood of refugees.

The Fulham Road, Gordon Road, Gay Street institutions, and the Hackney Casual Ward were swiftly cleared and prepared. The Empress Hall at Earl's Court and the Crystal Palace were taken over. By working day and night the ice-rink at Earl's Court was stripped of its tiers of seats and partitioned off into sections. The actual rink was drained and converted into a dining-hall and recreation-room. Kitchen equipment was installed and a miniature 30-bed hospital fitted up. Every possible step was taken to provide food, rest and a friendly reception for the people who were fleeing before the Nazi invasion.

The first party of refugees arrived on 14th May 1940, and thereafter they continued to arrive by day and night. The arrangements for their reception worked smoothly, even though on this occasion the Social Welfare Committee was dealing with a more terrible problem than destitution. Many of the refugees arrived in a pitiable condition. Women and children who had fled along the choked roads of France, with no respite from the terror of the Panzers pressing swiftly behind them, machine-gunned ruthlessly from the air, often without food and without sleep, driven on by a desperate urge to reach the haven which lay beyond the English Channel. There were children who had seen their parents die in the ditch beside them and had been caught up and swept on by another party of refugees. There were aged women who had seen their homes in French and Belgian villages crumble into sudden ruins and who had found a sudden desperate endurance in their aged limbs.

There were large family parties who came through with their possessions strapped in vast trunks and bundles carried between them. There were families who had set out on the crowded roads of France and had been diminished one by one until only a young girl or an old man had reached England. There were people swollen to gargantuan size by the many sets of clothing they were wearing and there were others who had no more than the light summer dresses they were wearing.

There were men and women who were too broken by their experiences to help themselves. There were men and women whose main thought was to get the weapons to carry on the fight. They poured into the centres by day and night, pitiable, tragic, broken, angry, tearful, defiant. They had crossed the Channel with returning

Social Welfare in Wartime

troopships; they had found space on the crowded decks of British warships; they had come across in crowded Bretagne fishing smacks; they had crowded perilously into tiny boats and rowed desperately for a day and a night towards the white cliffs of England. They had paddled across in their canvas canoes; they had improvised strange rafts and pushed out into the Channel to be picked up by our questing Channel patrols.

There were not only French, Belgium, Dutch, the people of the Allied Nations, but a great number of other nationalities had fled before the storm. There were Spanish Republicans, German anti-Nazis, Americans, Cubans, Czechs, Italians, Latvians, Lithuanians, Portuguese, Russians, and Turks. The refugees who passed through the reception centres comprised the people of forty-one nations. In the minds of the ordinary people of many nations there was little neutrality so far as the Nazis were concerned.

Then the sweep of the Nazi Panzers reached the Channel ports and the flood of refugees died down to a mere trickle. But that trickle continued until the day the British and American armies burst out of the Normandy beach-head and swept forward to the liberation of the Continent.

All through the war the Channel remained for thousands the highroad to freedom. There was no road too long, no suffering too intense, no difficulties too insurmountable to stop the men and women who made their way across the Channel to Britain. They found their way across a hostile continent; they broke out of prisons and escaped from the torture-chambers of the Gestapo. They were men and women who came to fight, or who had dragged their tortured bodies to die, in the last citadel of freedom left in Europe. A very large number of those who endured that strange and terrible odyssey were received and cared for during their first days in Britain in the reception centres of the L.C.C.

During the war years there were many other classes of people for whom the L.C.C. had to supply temporary care and accommodation. Over 10,000 of the troops evacuated from Dunkirk were provided with temporary billets in June 1940. After them came the people who were evacuated from the special defence areas on our coasts. Women enemy aliens found temporary accommodation at L.C.C. centres on their way to internment camps. In June 1940, too, Gibraltar was stripped for defence and the Council received the 3,500 civilian evacuees from the Rock. The centres were prepared in this case for a stay of considerable duration. Recreation rooms, nurseries, workrooms and household equipment and personal necessities were provided. New dietaries were instituted to meet the needs of people who were accustomed to very different food from the average English fare. The Gibraltarians settled down, on the whole, quite happily in a climate and surroundings which were very different from those of their native rock.

As " D-Day " approached the Council again prepared to receive an incoming flood of refugees. Among other centres, the whole of Onslow Square was taken over and prepared for their reception, but the Allied armies burst out of their Normandy bridgehead and swept so swiftly across France that the anticipated refugee problem did not arise. In fact, only eighty-five people were received from across the Channel.

Almost immediately an urgent use was found for the vacant accommodation in Onslow Square. It was used to house the workers who were brought to London from all over the country to undertake the repair of houses damaged in the flying bomb attacks which began on 13th June 1944.

Social Welfare in Wartime

More than any other administrative service of the L.C.C. the Social Welfare staff have seen the suffering and tragedy which the war brought to the men, women and children of all nations. For many refugees the friendly reception at the L.C.C. centres was their first introduction to Britain. The Social Welfare Department held out the welcoming hand at the threshold at a time when London was the cosmopolis of freedom.

CHAPTER XIV

WAR OVER THE HOSPITALS

THE great hospital system of the London County Council, with its 100 hospitals, containing some 72,000 beds and with a staff of 30,000, proved of inestimable value to London in the time of need.

I have already described how during the five years leading up to the outbreak of war these hospitals were modernised and re-equipped. As early as 1935 the Council began to formulate plans for the hospitals to be used as casualty clearing stations and base hospitals in the event of a national emergency. From 1938 onwards preparations were intensified, and at the time of the Munich crisis over 16,000 beds were available for air-raid casualties. This accommodation had been made available by re-equipping 10 fever hospitals and other institutions with the operating theatres and apparatus necessary for a general hospital, and by increasing the number of beds in the wards above the peace-time standards.

On the ambulance side, recruiting for the Auxiliary Ambulance Service began in March 1938, and by the end of September 1938 over 800 voluntary drivers had been enrolled. Protected emergency telephone switchboards were installed and 534 vehicles had been selected for ambulance purposes, and arrangements made for the adaption of 300 coaches and 69 school ambulances.

At the request of the Ministry of Health equipment was purchased by the Council for ambulance trains to be staffed by the medical and nursing staff of the School Medical Service.

The main features of the Council's own emergency

scheme for its hospitals had been completed when the Government began the preparation of the Emergency Hospitals Scheme which was to come into operation at the outbreak of war. Under the scheme the Government took partial control of all hospitals of any size and determined how many beds should be reserved for E.M.S. cases, that is civilian war casualties, service patients and A.R.P. personnel. Beds reserved for E.M.S. cases were paid for by the Government both when occupied or un-occupied, the rate of course being higher when occupied.

From an administrative point of view the Government's Emergency Hospital Scheme in London was open to a certain amount of criticism. In preparing the Scheme an undue amount of consideration had been given to preserving the interests and the susceptibilities of the voluntary hospitals at the expense in several instances of administrative efficiency. Greater London, for example, was divided into ten sections without consideration to Local Government areas or the relative size of the sectors, the guiding consideration being that at least one of the large voluntary teaching hospitals should be in each sector. A staff member of the voluntary hospitals was usually placed in charge of these sectors, few of whom had any experience of hospital administration, except possibly within the limited fields of their own single hospital, while the vast administrative experience of the Council's staff was not used to any comparable extent, even though the Council's hospitals were responsible for 76 out of every 100 beds earmarked under the scheme.

There were other criticisms which might be made of the Emergency Hospital Scheme, but none the less the Council and its staff worked without stint or reserve to ensure the efficient operation of the scheme and to maintain the highest possible standards of medical and surgical attention for the E.M.S. cases which came into the care of the Council's hospitals.

The war placed immense burdens on the municipal hospitals. Apart from the treatment of air-raid casualties, the municipal hospitals maintained without interruption their treatment of sick and injured. In 1940, for example, over 150,000 patients were admitted to the Council's hospitals and nearly a million people received out-patient treatment. In the same year 43,000 operations were performed and 630,000 treatments by massage and electrical equipment were given. Nearly 200,000 X-ray films were used and 380,000 examinations were carried out in the hospital laboratories. There were over 14,000 confinements in the maternity wards and 100,000 attendances at the ante-natal clinics. During that same year, 1940, over 46,000 patients received treatment under the District Medical Services and the District Nursing Service made 100,000 visits to patients in their own homes, apart from 114,000 separate visits to administer insulin. The Domiciliary Midwife Service dealt with 12,007 confinements and the ambulance service carried 135,745 patients, apart from air-raid casualties.

These large figures convey some slight impression of the calls which were made on the municipal hospitals and their allied services during a critical year. The whole range of these services was maintained over a period when as many as nine hospitals were out of commission and an overall total of 14,600 beds were put out of use by enemy action. In these circumstances, during the war years not only have the great majority of the civilian sick in London been treated in L.C.C. hospitals, but these hospitals have dealt with nearly one half of the air-raid casualties admitted to hospital in London. It was a feat without parallel in the history of hospital administration.

War over the Hospitals

In this short account it is not possible to give anything like an adequate picture of the immense difficulties which the Council's hospitals faced and overcame. Here, however, is the brief account of what happened at one L.C.C. hospital.

Early in September 1940 a large bomb demolished a ward block. Fortunately the block was not occupied at the time as it had been cleared to allow the windows to be protected—the next day these wards would have been filled with patients. In the darkness, while the raid was still on, all the staff assisted in moving patients in adjoining blocks to safer parts of the hospital. When daylight came emergency repairs were started and by nightfall essential repairs to the rest of the hospital had been completed. The next day clearance of debris was commenced and equipment was salvaged from the damaged block. The medical superintendent reported, " We are carrying on and can resume admissions in forty-eight hours."

A fortnight later another H.E. bomb demolished the laundry and boiler-house. The three stokers who were in the boiler-house escaped through scalding steam and water to safety. On that occasion the hot water and steam services were cut off and the electric generator put out of action, so it was decided to evacuate the hospital. A member of the L.C.C. visiting this hospital at dawn found the patients, old and young alike, sitting wrapped in blankets, as cheerful as could be, enjoying a meal from the field kitchens provided by the Council for just such an emergency.

Three weeks later the hospital was again in use, but within ten days another bomb severely damaged one block. The main gas and water services were cut off, and once again the hospital had to be evacuated. By the same incredible luck there were once again no casualties. Within a fortnight the admission of patients was resumed, but within a week the hospital sustained another direct hit. There were again no casualties. The emergency arrangements were such, however, that on this occasion, the admission of patients was continued on the following day.

This account of what happened at one hospital had its counterpart so far as several other hospitals were concerned. Nearly every one of the Council's one hundred hospitals suffered damage during the war, some of them on several occasions. In those cases where severe damage was sustained many problems of re-organisation had to be swiftly tackled. Patients had to be moved to safer parts of the hospital, or evacuated to other hospitals, sometimes outside London. The inter-hospital transport, organised by the Ministry of Health and the London Regional Headquarters, worked efficiently on all these occasions.

There were in the Council's hospitals, however, many patients for whom the voluntary and other hospitals could not provide accommodation—for example, mental cases and tuberculosis patients. When emergency evacuations were carried out these patients had to be distributed to other L.C.C. hospitals where beds for such cases were available. It was only the vast ramifications of a comprehensive hospital organisation which enabled the Council to cope with the demands presented on these occasions.

Another major problem of the war years was the sharp increase in the demand for the accommodation of the chronic sick, particularly at the onset of the Blitz. The evacuation and the break-up of homes through the military call-up left a large number of chronically sick people without anyone to provide them with proper care. In September 1940 the influx of these cases into the hos-

War over the Hospitals

pitals was so heavy that the pressure was only relieved by the Government undertaking the mass evacuation of 4,000 of these cases. The relief, however, proved temporary, for this type of case continued to seek admission to such an extent that certain acute hospitals had to be utilised for their accommodation.

There were many other spheres in which the municipal hospitals made their contribution to the war effort. The pioneer work carried out by the Council in peace in establishing its pathological laboratories proved of great value, not only to London, but to the whole nations at war. The sera and vaccines manufactured in the Council's laboratories were supplied to many sources, including the national pool of the Medical Research Council, the Colonies and the Egyptian Government. In addition, the " media " laboratories of the Council provided on the outbreak of war not only the needs of all the laboratories in the London region but also a large proportion of the needs of the British Army. The Council later extended these supplies to meet the requirements of all the Government laboratories in Great Britain, as well as supplying a large part of the needs of the American and Canadian armies in this country.

The urgent demands of wartime did not lead to the ending of the Council's contributions to medical research. The British Post-Graduate Medical School at Hammersmith had continued to provide facilities for research. Among many other subjects, a careful investigation was carried out of the comparative effects of a radium beam and X-rays in the treatment of cancer of the mouth and throat.

The Council's hospital also performed very valuable services to the cause of medical education during the war. The practical training of senior students in the voluntary hospitals was abruptly interfered with by the almost complete evacuation of these hospitals at the outbreak of war and by their policy of severely restricting the admission of new patients. A very large number of students were able to continue their interrupted training in the L.C.C. hospitals. At the request of the deans of the voluntary teaching hospitals the Council undertook in its own hospitals the training of the medical students in obstetrics, gynaecology, fever cases and psychiatry. In short, over a wide field of medical education the municipal hospitals had become the centres of student training and post-graduate work in London.

For the other emergency services of the Council there were weeks and sometimes months of respite from heavy pressure. For the hospitals, however, there was no temporary relaxation of effort. The pressure of the sick and injured in the municipal hospitals imposed an immense and continuing strain on their resources at a period when the shortage of medical, nursing and domestic staff was becoming more and more acute with each succeeding month.

The attack by the V-weapons brought a new period of intense strain and anxiety for all connected with the hospital services. Almost the first flying bomb to fall in London damaged St. Clement's Hospital at Bow. During the V attack the hospitals were involved in 138 incidents—101 by V1 and 37 by V2. Six hospitals were so badly damaged that they had to be completely evacuated. St. Olave's Hospital, Bermondsey, which had been damaged in the Blitz, was damaged no less than seven times by V1 and V2 missiles.

In August 1944 the Government decided that patients should be evacuated from hospitals in London. This task was undertaken by the Council and the Ministry of Health and in just over 14 days more than 13,000 patients were transferred to the North of England.

War over the Hospitals

During the war from 1939 to 1945, the Council's hospitals accommodated 20,000 air-raid casualties, 13,200 during the Blitz and 6,800 during the V-raids.

The number of patients who were killed by enemy action in the Council's hospitals were 200 in the Blitz and 33 in the V-raids. Forty-four of the hospitals' medical, nursing and general staff were killed in the Blitz and 15 in the later attacks.

No record of the L.C.C. hospitals in war would be complete without some account of the courage and devotion to duty of the hospitals' staff during the period of the savage attacks on London. During the whole of those war years every member of the medical, nursing, domestic and other staff thought and acted with the overriding consideration of the safety and welfare of their patients always before them.

Many awards for bravery and devotion to duty were won by all ranks in the hospital service. Possibly, typical of the selfless disregard for danger of the nursing staffs was the action which won Staff Nurse Ruby Rosser the George Medal.

On 19th November, 1940, a high explosive bomb struck a ward block where Nurse Rosser was on duty, penetrating all three floors and exploding in a room on the ground floor. Nurse Rosser immediately rushed to the bedside of the patient who was in the room where the explosion occurred and protected her body and head from flying fragments. She remained at her post by this patient until it was possible for the patient and herself to be rescued through a window, despite the fact that the ceiling of the ground floor ward, together with the floor and equipment of the ward above continued to fall into the room on top of both of them.

That is one citation from the long list of awards won by the staff of the hospital services. But for every one who won the honours of battle, there were a thousand whose courage and devotion went unrecorded in any official account. The doctors whose skill and devotion never faltered, the matrons whose calm courage was the inspiration of staff and patients alike, the domestic staffs who carried out their jobs with quiet competence in situations of extreme danger, and, above all, the nurses, who in the midsts of wards of sick and apprehensive people displayed what was possibly the greatest courage and devotion of all.

On the morning of 28th March 1945, a flying bomb passed over the Queen Mary's Hospital at Sidcup and exploded in Scadbury Park, breaking a few windows. Four people were brought in for treatment to the casualty department of Queen Mary's Hospital. These were the last air-raid casualties in London, and the haphazard flying bomb which fell in Scadbury Park was the last enemy missile to fall in Britain in the Second World War.

CHAPTER XV

THE LABOUR BOROUGHS OF LONDON

THERE are many gaps in this account of the work of the Labour Majority on the London County Council. A great deal of inconspicuous but important work for London has not been recorded. It has not been possible to compress into a few hundred pages anything like a complete account of those ten crowded and tumultuous years.

I have described the developments in the Council's services at the level at which they touched the lives and activities of Londoners. I have tried to show how in 1934 a new social impulse took hold of those services and began to project its influence into the lives, the health, the education, the well-being and happiness of countless thousands of Londoners who may never have suspected that a new influence was powerfully at work.

In a few pages, too, I have tried to tell something of the way the peace-time services of the Council—the schools, the hospitals, the social welfare services—were shaped by the urgent pressures of war. I have given a brief account of the Council's heavy responsibilities for the Civil Defence of London, and I have tried to show how the Council handled the tremendous new problems which were thrust upon it by the swift emergencies of war.

But a great deal has perforce been left out. No attempt has been made to assess the imprint of personalities on developments. The energetic leadership of Herbert Morrison during the years of peace-time progress, and the outstanding competence with which his successor, Lord Latham, carried the immense responsibilities which fell to him as Leader of the Council during the years of war. The unremitting work of Charles Robertson as chairman of the Education Committee. The heavy task which fell to Dr. Somerville Hastings in building up the new municipal hospital services; the untiring resolution with which Lewis Silkin and C. W. Gibson grappled with the immense problems involved in sweeping away the London slums, and the work of I. J. Heyward in shaping the new social welfare services. It must be left to later and fuller accounts to assess what London owes to these, and many other councillors, committee members and officers of the Council, who during the long and anxious years worked untiringly for the welfare and protection of this great city and all its citizens.

There is another conspicuous omission. This account of municipal progress in London has been devoted to the activities of the London County Council. But there are in London twenty-eight Borough Councils which possess very important powers in the fields of housing, public health, sanitation, and for the provision of public baths, parks and other amenities. As we have seen in Chapter II, the Act of 1899 which created the London Boroughs did not seek to make them partners in the task of governing London. The Balfour Act aimed at creating for London an "aggregate of municipalities", each managing its own affairs and fostering its own local loyalties, and together exercising a compelling drag on the "socialist and collectivist experiments" of the London County Council.

But it is impossible to halt indefinitely the impulse towards social progress. When it was cast out of the County Council it began to thrust its way powerfully into the chambers of the Borough Councils. Battersea, Bermondsey, Greenwich, Deptford and Poplar were among the first Borough Councils to have Labour

The Labour Boroughs of London

majorities. After the Borough Council elections in November 1934 fifteen Labour Borough Councils were able to join hands with the Labour L.C.C. in the task of accelerating the pace of municipal progress in London. The 1937 elections increased the number of Labour Boroughs to seventeen.[1]

It was possibly with regard to housing that the co-operation between the Labour Boroughs and the Labour County Council yielded the most important results. The Borough Councils had no powers to build outside their own areas, so that unless they could secure some vacant land or a suitable clearance area many Labour Councils who had been eager to tackle their own slum areas had been handicapped in their slum-clearance schemes. The brake of these limitations disappeared when the Labour Boroughs were able to join hands with the Labour L.C.C. in the great slum-clearance drive which was launched in 1934. In fact, once this slum clearance programme was under way several Labour Boroughs, like Deptford and Camberwell, confined themselves to small housing schemes and left the big schemes in their areas to the greater resources of the L.C.C. Other Labour Boroughs, like Battersea, volunteered to act as " decanting areas ", the dwellings built by the Borough Council being used to house tenants from areas cleared by the L.C.C.

Although most of the major slum-clearance schemes were left to the L.C.C., the contribution of the Labour Boroughs to the total of slum clearance in London was not insignificant in itself. In the five years leading up to the outbreak of war the Labour Boroughs in London provided 8,472 dwellings, compared with 2,418 dwellings provided by the non-Labour boroughs.

[1] At the Borough Council elections in November 1945, Labour captured 23 Boroughs.

The standards and amenities of this housing programme did not fall behind those of the County Council. The flats built by Hackney, Fulham, Woolwich and other Labour Boroughs had lifts, sun balconies, communal laundries and drying-rooms. Special children's playgrounds, community centres and infant welfare centres were also provided by Labour Borough Councils on some of their estates.

Public health was a field in which the Labour Boroughs did not have to wait for the co-ordinating influence of a Labour L.C.C. The return of a Labour majority on a Borough Council has meant in every case a very rapid extension of the local public health and welfare services. Bermondsey, for example, provided a maternity and child-welfare centre within a half-mile of every home in the borough. Southwark provided 11 maternity and child welfare clinics, and supplemented them with a successful scheme for full-time home helps and holidays for mothers, particularly after child-birth. Most of the Labour Boroughs had employed panels of home helpers a long time before the introduction of the official scheme during the war.

Heart clinics, convalescent homes, toddlers' clinics, dental clinics, solaria, clinics for eye, ear and throat complaints, special clinics for women, diphtheria immunisation centres—this short list gives some idea of the comprehensive range of public health services provided by the Labour Boroughs of London.

The thoroughness with which the Labour Boroughs in London used their public health powers is reflected in the annual report of their medical officers of health. Bermondsey, for example, was captured by Labour in 1922. Within twelve years the death-rate in Bermondsey had been cut by no less than 34 per cent. The infant death-rate was reduced year by year from 159 to 37 per

The Labour Boroughs of London

thousand births. The death-rate from infectious diseases was cut by 85 per cent., and by 1933 the maternal death-rate in Bermondsey at 2·5 per thousand was below the average for the whole of Britain.

There are many other statistics which show the effectiveness of the Labour Boroughs' work. Before the war the infant mortality rates in every Labour Borough were coming down, while in Tory Boroughs the infant death-rate had actually risen. The maternity death-rates were steadily reduced and the death-rate from tuberculosis in several Labour Boroughs was halved.

The extensive public health services provided by the Labour Boroughs have made an immense contribution to the improvement in the health of the metropolis.

The Labour Boroughs made full use of their powers to improve the amenities of their districts. Public libraries and baths, communal laundries equipped with electrically operated washing-machines, parks and playgrounds, community centres and advice bureaux are a few of the many services and amenities which the Labour Boroughs have provided for their districts. Before the war eleven Labour Boroughs operated their own municipal electricity undertakings, and they were the pioneers of free and assisted wiring schemes which brought electricity within reach of many thousands who could not previously have paid the high charges for installation.

In brief, the Labour Boroughs were the energetic partners of the Labour County Council in working for the municipal betterment of London.

This account must close at a time when London is facing the immense problems of reconstruction. The housing of its people is only the foremost of a formidable array of problems which have arisen to clamour and press for attention. And behind the problems of physical reconstruction the old, familiar question of the "government of London" presents itself with a new and compelling urgency. At the heart of all problems of reconstruction in London is the need for securing the machinery and powers for tackling the immense tasks which must be carried out if London is to become a more convenient, healthier and far better place for all its citizens.

As the last pages of this book are written the return of a Labour Government has made the prospect of a better London appear more certain than it has ever been. Many of the problems and difficulties which have burdened the previous pages undoubtedly will prove more tractable. The London County Council elections in 1934 ushered in a decade of far-reaching municipal progress in London. There is now every prospect that the progress of that decade will be outpaced by the ten years which lie ahead.

The decision about the future rests very largely with the citizens of London. Nearly everything in this book points to the fact that a local government election is not an isolated event in the life of a modern community. The London County Council can exercise an enormous influence on the lives of all who live within the County of London. The quality of our local government, the policies and outlook of our councillors are undoubtedly among the most important influences in our associated lives.

Once before in the history of London there came an opportunity of building a great and splendid city. But the noble plans of Sir Christopher Wren were thrust aside by the jostling scramble of civic greed and narrow self-interests. We stand at the gateway of a new opportunity. It is within our power to use this new opportunity so that future generations walking our streets shall say that we built worthily and well.

15*th November*, 1945.

For Product Safety Concerns and Information please contact our EU
representative GPSR@taylorandfrancis.com
Taylor & Francis Verlag GmbH, Kaufingerstraße 24, 80331 München, Germany

www.ingramcontent.com/pod-product-compliance
Lightning Source LLC
Chambersburg PA
CBHW071828300426
44116CB00009B/1473